Society Driven Design
co-creating brighter futures - a practitioners handbook

For Xavier, Caspian & Tallulah
forever in beautiful conversations - spanning across space, time and love - in the world that lives within, and the next

Overview

In 1971, at the height of the Vietnam War and at a time of great political and social instability, Dutch philosopher Fons Elders invited Noam Chomsky and Michel Foucault to take part in a televised debate. The debate took place at Eindhoven University of Technology in the Netherlands and focused on the theme of human nature. Two of the twentieth century's most influential public intellectuals, sharing their thoughts on hidden power and the legalities of better justice. Throughout the discussion, Chomsky reiterated a high regard for the structures, rules and principles found in language.

"An adult, speaker, who has somehow acquired an amazing range of abilities, which enable him in particular to say what he means, to understand what people say to him, to do this in a fashion that I think is proper to call highly creative[1]."

To communicate with another person is to engage in a highly creative process.

For the designer to facilitate change they must be willing to embark on their own transformational journey. Travelling to the places where design rarely goes, the edges of our society, in order to host conversations across space, time and culture.

Life is messy. Society is complex. Phenomena is non-linear. Poverty is about more than just money. We cannot design 'think' our way out of these challenges.

The use of applied design in tackling social inequalities has become more popular in recent years. In some quarters this growth has preceded the commodification of the design process, and as such, design is more vulnerable to over functionalism. The growing silhouette of the design toolkit is in danger of eclipsing the craft of design itself.

---

[1] Noam Chomsky debates with Michel Foucault 1971 https://chomsky.info/1971xxxx/

The over dependency on design tools disables my ability to reason with humanity as a designer. I do not mean to diminish the value of design tools, I am simply seeking a different way to share my practice. To that end, this is not an academic book that seeks to engage your mind, but a practitioner's declaration written for the heart.

This is a book about society driving its own change.
Change that is facilitated by the soulful designer through meaningful conversations.

Conversations that will take the designer on an interior journey, one that leads to themselves, their practice and their own definition of design. Travelling to the margins of our communities and the depths of ourselves - in doing so the designer will become fluent in the language of hope and loss.

Society driven design brings all the components of a collaborative conversation together like an exploded drawing. Conversations that will foster long term collaborations. Collaborations that will continue beyond the projects that we will make together - the art of the Social License.

I will be exploring three areas that significantly contribute to the practice of socially driven design throughout the book. The role of the designer. The art of conversations. The value of the Social License.

As an example of the society driven design process, I will be sharing the extraordinary story of InHouse Records. The worlds first functioning record label to have been co-created in a UK prison which has led to incredibly low recidivism rates.

I sincerely hope this practitioners handbook will become a meaningful addition to your library and your heartfelt practice.

The designer. The conversation. The Social License.

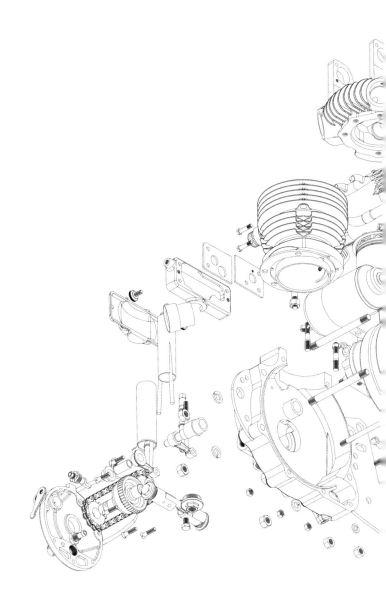

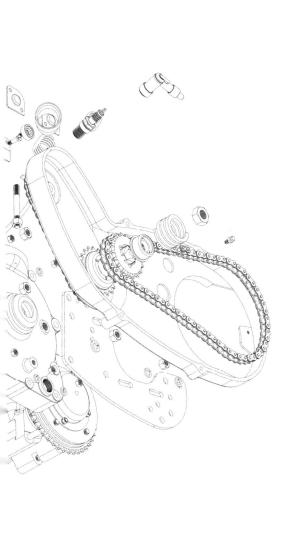

acknowledgments

Editor: Tallulah Mae Armani
Cover Art: Hannah Lee

special thanks

The Guild - Neil Sartorio, Justin W. Cook, Nick De Leon and Atsushi Hasagawa

Grace, Carl and ALL at InHouse Records - keep it 101 - binary.
Daisy, Bex, Abbie, Lance, Andy D, Sara P for making this happen!
Sarah Lockhart and my Epic UK family - Changing the game.
Captain Phil Nugent, Rafäl, Nico, Roman and Antonio - One of these, one of these and a yoghurt.

Jim Chancellor, the prince of the music industry.
Richard, John, Carolyn, Nicolas and Qian - my RCA family.
Professor Clive Grinyer - Football Love, Jazz Clubs and world changing.

Kelly Jones - conversations across space, time and culture - with pasta.
Joel Pott - the king of invisible sacrifices.
Ben Drew - for the inspirational sacrifice of Each One Teach One.
Jamie Lenman - you are a master craftsman and a true gentleman.
Makepeace - Forza Fora!! (you too Cala) - friendship and change.
Mary V. Mullin and all at the Sir Misha Black Awards.
Thomas Horton - Grand Avenues is society driven design.
Naomi, Matt, Paul and all at Catch22 - The original Trequartistas - changing from within.
Toban Shadlyn - practice building, hope forming conversations.
Rob & Emily at Ecological Citizens - greener conversations!
Hannah Steiner and all at EY - your energy, kindness and support.
Cormac Russell - The champion of ABCD and connected communities.
The Sherer's, the Annis', the Campbell's and Steely - From Brighton with love - thank you for journeying through the good, the tough and the beautiful.
Andrew Marshall - Carlowrie and Astell.

Llulah Mae, words fail me, but thankfully not you - you are a genius.
Harm, Soraya and Peter at BiS for your faith, compassion and patience.

SP for teaching me to see the person, not the prison.
We had to do a mad 'ting.
We changed the game, we changed the pattern.
Thats why I gotta thank him.

Society Driven Design

co-creating brighter futures - a practitioners handbook

Hoda Judah Armani
Edited by Tallulah Mae Armani

BiS Publishers

Conversation | ˌkɒnvəˈseɪʃn |
noun

a talk, especially an informal one, between two or more people, in which news and ideas are exchanged.

ORIGIN
Middle English (in the sense 'living among, familiarity, intimacy'): via Old French from Latin conversatio(n-), from the Latin verb conversari 'keep company (with'), from con- 'with' + versare, frequentative of vertere 'to turn'. The current sense of the verb dates from the early 17th century.

Introduction
A Practitioners Handbook 13

Endings
Introduction 23
Design 24
Relationship 38
Endings 63

Transitions
Introduction 72
Understanding Phenomena 73
Understanding Conversations 101
Understanding the Social License 115

Beginnings
Introduction 171
Insights 172
Theories and Assumptions 183
Conditions for Change 191
Designing Meaning 198

Transitioning
Designer 227
Conversations 228
The Social License 229
InHouse Records 234
Total Design 235
Respect 238
The Reflection at Folies-Bergère 240

1

11

INTRODUCTION

Introduction

Things end.

Perhaps this is the hardest phenomena we all wrestle with.
From the trivial to the profound, all things end.

Generally, we tend not to talk about endings, perhaps this is because
we do not feel adequately equipped to cope with the sadness that
encompasses finite conclusions, or maybe it's that endings draw us to
the edges of our vocabulary, where our language lexicon becomes raw,
unable to express the depth of our emotions - tongue tied. We become
lost for words.

On the other hand however, we are able to speak with emotional
fluency about beginnings. 'New' is attractive, 'new' provides hope,
possibilities, it is endless. In fact, the abundance of 'new' means we do
not need to think too much, if at all, about 'endings'.
Upgrade. Improve. Modernise. Customise.

Fluent in the language of 'new', yet largely illiterate in the language of
loss. Perhaps we find ourselves so unbalanced because it's harder to
sell 'endings' as successfully as we do 'beginnings'? Maybe we are
unable to fully comprehend the language of beginnings unless we truly
know the language of endings? What if, in pursuit of building better
beginnings, we need to learn how to build better endings?

From the trivial to the profound, all things end.

However, the ending of something, isn't necessarily the ending of
everything; the end of a marriage isn't the end of love and the end of a
journey, isn't the end of adventure.

Before we can be confident in designing new things, we need to master
the craft of designing endings and designing them well. Over the last
twenty years my design practice has led me to collaborate with people
caught in some of the most challenging circumstances imaginable, and

successfully speaking about endings was often the catalyst to imagine new beginnings. If we desire change, we must collaborate; oppression can only be eliminated with the participation of the oppressed. Poverty can only be eradicated with the collaboration of the poor. In order to collaborate we must be able to see preferred futures together and to realise this, we must learn the language of loss and speak well of endings.

Therefore, society driven design can only truly begin when we design meaningful conversations about endings. Before we design anything, we must design conversations.

Designing better conversations about endings and beginnings is unavailing if we are not collaborating. Collaboration is transition; for any ending to progress toward successful beginnings there must be a transition. I have learnt - often the hard way - that homelessness is not just about the homeless, nor is prison just about the prisoner. We all have a stake in our society and thus, for society to drive design meaningfully, we must design better transitions and thus, better ways for all to engage.

The world is run by those who show up and I invite you all to show up.

I am minded to paraphrase John Ruskin's 1872 *Law of Help*[2]: "The collaboration of all things across everywhere in order to sustain life." Ruskin saw in nature the essential alliances that need to be created by all, in order to sustain life. He argued that such a law should be applied to human development, indeed alliances must be sought by everyone, across everywhere, in order to sustain life. All life is transitioning.

Establishing alliances require us to find effective ways of engaging with wide and diverse neighbourhoods. Before we can design anything, we are designing conversations - conversations about endings and conversations about transitions.

---

[2] John Ruskin, Modern Painters, Volume 5, 1860 John Wiley and Sons

The social designer must become skilled at designing conversations, in order to reach all and, to speak of endings that lead to collaborations, transitions and virtuous beginnings.

This is a book about social change driven by a new kind of collaboration. As such, I seek to frame the role of design and the practice of the designer, as an internal journey as well as an external process.

I will share principles and conditions for making conversations that facilitate transitions through engagement, clearly communicate endings and as a result, foster better beginnings. Indeed it has been my privilege to have shared beautiful conversations about endings and effective transitions through collaboration with many communities who have designed their own beginnings. In the process of pursuing my practice, I have created my own circular zig-zag vocational pathway of social transformation - endings, transitions, beginnings and transitions once more.

Perhaps with hindsight, it would have been easier if I were to chart a more direct route for my practice - avoiding the serpentine heartache - but that would have come at the expense of foregoing failure, which, not only seems impossible to me, is also undesirable. The absence of failure would effectively rob me of the rocket fuel needed for transformation; both personally and societally. Indeed experiencing endings and talking about them honestly, can help us **all** transition to designing better beginnings.

Certainly in my own life, I can testify to the difficulty of attempting to pursue societal change without being open to personal change. Let me be clear, it doesn't work. It's impossible to live in one world, whilst trying to breathe in another. Many have tried, none to my knowledge have succeeded.

From the trivial to the profound, all things end.

In Shakespeare's *Hamlet*, Polonius cautions his son, Laertes, to be honest with himself: "This above all, to thine own self be true.[3]" Before we design anything, we must design honest conversations with ourselves - transitional dialogue. The designer seeking social change, must desire change in their own lives. Personal change facilitates growth, which in turn often signifies the ending of unwanted things in our life.

All things end. This is a good thing, for bad things.
From injustice to poverty, these too, will end.
Design, I have found, has a significant role in helping unwanted things to end quicker.

Impact in society happens best when society drives it and for that to happen, collaboration becomes essential. However, diverse collaborations and meaningful endings, need effective dialogue to inspire and empower a society to design change. For society to drive positive change, we must learn to design endings through conversations where all can contribute. Without designing endings, we are unable to collaborate effectively and thus transitioning becomes problematic, rendering our beginnings as suboptimal.

We all have a role to play and we can all make a difference to this world.

In fact, a significant motivation for writing this book has been the sheer number of people over the last twenty years, who have asked me for advice regarding how they can make a difference to our society.

From meeting people who are serving prison sentences to folk living in absolute poverty, I have learnt, all people want to make a difference. People in the midst of their own unresolved and incredibly challenging circumstances, choose to see the wellbeing of others as an important part of their own lives. How can that not reinforce anyone's hope in humanity? Of course I have met many who are not in challenging

---

[3] William Shakespeare, Hamlet, 2003 Penguin Classics, UK

circumstances but still their empathy moves them to compassion as they too ask the same question of themselves, how can they make a difference in the world.

By doing what we all do everyday, just better, we are all able to participate in creating better conversations; better conversations that lead to a better understanding of ourselves and of each other. Better conversations that can further collaborations across neighbourhoods and communities in order to establish society driven design. In the spirit of Ruskin; we should be designing conversations that advance alliances in support of sustaining all life. Herbert Simon once said: "Everyone designs who devises courses of action aimed at changing existing situations into preferred ones.[4]" We all have the capacity to change things for the better, no matter how big or small, therefore the designer in us all must be freed.

The first movement of this book begins with an ending, exploring the internal journey for the designer. In socially driven design, the internal journey bears a critical influence on the outcome of the process, therefore we will be exploring this journey through three lenses. How we define design, our relationship to design and how this forms and informs our fluency in the language of loss and endings. I will be making a case for the work of society driven design to be viewed as a craft and thus, the role of the designer as a craftsman - one that can speak the language of endings through the craft of design.

The second movement entitled transitions is an external practice of understanding. I will be sharing how the majority of my time in the design process is spent in transitions and the importance of understanding over knowledge throughout the journey. This movement possesses three overarching themes: how to make sense of phenomena, how to make sense of conversations and the application of both within the Social License, a new approach to the art of collaboration. I will focus on how we can make the space for a different kind of collaboration - no longer about transitioning, but about making - the kind of space that champions change.

---

4 Herbert Simon, The Sciences of the Artificial, 1970, MIT Press

I will be sharing a pathway for collaboration to transcend a 'means to an end approach' by making the collaboration itself the destination. In this way the value of the Social License becomes far greater than any initiative it may birth. We will examine organisational structures for collaboration and explore with greater detail how we may embark upon hosting multiple Social Licenses. Licenses that represent communities within pre-determined systems and those who fall outside of any recognised system. I will also be sharing stories of socially driven initiatives spanning across my two decade practice within the phenomena of homelessness and the criminal justice system.

The third movement entitled, beginnings, features the story of InHouse Records, the groundbreaking work of a multi-award winning innovative education programme. I will be sharing the remarkable story of how an eduction programme became a programme for change, an utterly unique approach to learning, that is evidencing extraordinary outcomes. This third movement of the book covers four sections: understanding and insights, theories and assumptions, factors of change and designing meaning and measure. The sections have been carefully curated in order to profile the thinking and conversations that took place across the whole process.

The final movement is entitled, transitioning, in which I will summarise all the themes we have discussed throughout the book. Beginning with the end, a reminder of the interior journey we all need to embark upon if we are to navigate the exterior journey of design application. I will also share the first steps in building your own Social License.

Whilst this book has been written with service design students and practitioners in mind, as this is the iteration of design I lecture and practice in, I do hope the broader design world, and change makers may also find value across all four movements. It is my aspiration that this book may find a wider appeal with social entrepreneurs, third sector agencies fighting to innovate, and those working within local authorities, keen to strengthen the relationship with their local citizens.

This book is not an academic resource, but a living handbook for the socially driven designer - from one practitioner to another.

It is my intention for this book to enhance your collective practice and understanding. I have chosen to loosely follow a Socratic design process within the book because that is the process I have used in every prison, homeless shelter or challenging scenario I have found myself in across the world over the last twenty years. Making sense in order to make, is perhaps a naively simple maxim, but it is one that has enabled participants from prisons across the USA and UK, as well homeless communities from Chennai to London, to collaborate with maximum effect.

Ultimately, I hope that this book will be the source of creative hydration for all who thirst to make a difference in this world. For the designer specifically, I hope this book can support the growth of your own practice in the service of pursuing a better way to organise our society and, in the process, a better way of being human in the service of each other - better conversations about endings transitioning to better beginnings, by way of meaningful collaboration.

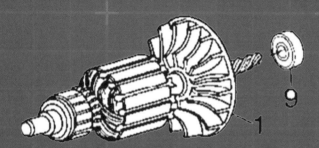

ENDINGS

Endings

Before we design anything, we must design conversations and before we design conversations, we must understand our own dimensions, our own aspirations and our own motivations. Before we can explore the application of society driven design, we must first study the internal journey.

In this first movement we will be examining the interior journey of the socially driven designer across three parts. Beginning with a definition of design, our relationship with design and the language of endings.

Defining socially driven design will require us to explore what we mean when we talk of design and the implications that any definition we draw upon, may have on the role of the socially driven designer.

Forming our own relationship with design will require us to introduce the concept of the designers practice. The space where our internal journey can meet our external application. We will discuss what responsibility the designer has to personal and professional improvement and how this can be made constant and sustainable. Toward the end of this theme, I will make the case for the relationship between the socially driven designer and design to be that of the craftsman and craft - investigating the attributes of craftsmanship for social change.

Finally we will be exploring how an articulation of our design practice, internal and external, contains the very vowels and consonants needed to speak the language of loss and endings.

Endings Part One
Design an Interior Journey

When I was nine years old, design revealed truth to me.

It was the first time I had seen an exploded drawing. A power drill, with all of its intricate components carefully sketched in a frozen floating state of suspension, captured at the moment just before it was about to be magically assembled. To the nine year old me, this drawing was truth, everything that was previously hidden had now been revealed. As if Bertolt Brecht had stepped into the design world, breaking down the fourth wall - making the consumer directly conscious of every component they had just purchased and not the illusion of the brand[5]. This intricate line drawing, made known the true relationship between the heterogeneous parts of the drill. A drawing that enabled owners to carry out repairs and maintain upkeep by understanding how it works.

I learnt at nine years old, that design can reveal things that are hidden, enabling us to see more clearly, facilitating repair and re-use.

Design can be truthful.

Twenty years later, I read Naomi Klein's book, *No Logo*[6].
It was the first time I had become aware of sinister supply chains and barbaric bonded labour. Famous brands choosing to make their garments in countries, that exercise weak employment governance, for pennies, in order to sell the same garments, in countries with stronger employment governance, for gargantuan profits. Making stuff, in places of extreme poverty, in order to sell it in places of extreme wealth. I learnt how the ubiquitous white t-shirt covered an army of abhorrent crimes.

---

[5] Bertolt Brecht, Brecht on Performance, 2018, Bloomsbury, UK

[6] Naomi Klein, No Logo, 1999, Picador, UK

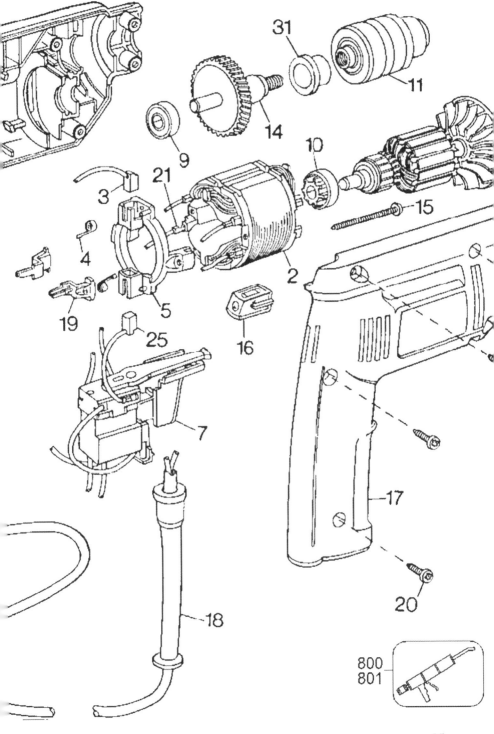

31

11

14

9

21

3

10

15

4

2

19

5

16

25

7

17

18

20

800
801

Supply chains have been designed, bonded labour has been designed. Orchestrating the outsourcing of manufacturing to places where their workforce are paid almost nothing and enjoy weaker governance, is a design process. Bill Moggridge, pioneering designer of our modern era said: "Few people think about this or are aware of it. But there is nothing made by human beings that does not involve a design decision somewhere.[7]" Everything that is man-made, has been designed, not just the artefacts, but the systems that control the workers, the governance that allows infringements of human rights, these too have all been designed.

I learnt at twenty nine years old, that design can hide things that are wrong, disabling us from seeing reality and facilitating the need for new.

Design can be deceptive.

Bad things have been covered up in order to sell seemingly good things. Things we don't necessarily need, but never the less things we are encouraged to want. New things.

New is necessary.

'New' is attractive, 'new' provides hope, possibilities - it is endless. In fact, 'new' means we do not need to think about 'endings'. Upgrade. Improve. Modernise. Customise. Consume. Design is used to sell, it's used to market and it's used to make.

Of course it would be ridiculous for me to lay the blame of consumerism with design. However design has been complicit with some of the darkest moments of our history whilst design has also contributed to some of the most breathtakingly positive moments of our society.

Design is not inherently truthful or deceptive; design can only be the embodiment of the designer.

---

[7] Bill Moggridge, Designing Interactions, 2006, MIT Press

How each designer chooses to define design will have a significant impact on what they design. Whilst this may seem an irrelevant exercise to some who occupy more long standing design disciplines, for those who are determined to apply design towards social change, the definition of design becomes imperative.

Design must be clear in its definition by the designer. Perhaps the designer needs to make explicit their definition of design as an act of the designer's civic responsibility and public accountability? Design is not inherently truthful or deceptive, the socially driven designer however, must be aware of their own values and motivations and to do this, a definition of design must be sought by the designer.

It's my belief and experience that design can advance our society in just and equitable ways. Over the last twenty years, I have met many designers and many design students, who want to see a better world; I am convinced their belief will ensure that design can truly become a force for good across our globe. What they and I believe, is that given the opportunity to design, society would also want to see better ways of being human. However if the motivation of the designer remains invisible, we will find genuine collaboration problematic. As we will explore further in the book, a binding principle of collaboration is honesty, and whilst there is an expectation for collaborators to be honest about their aspirations and hopes within the design process, so too must the designer be honest about their aspirations and hopes before collaborating with others.

Through the creation of meaningful and honest conversations, across space, time and culture, we are able, together, to make change.

If the design of an exploded drawing can reveal that which is hidden, enabling clarity of sight and facilitating repair and renewal, then surely design can make luminous supply chains that are fair and sustainable. Whatever has been made badly, can be re-made beautifully, reclaimed and re-designed better than it was before. Design can be truthful in its reveal of deception enabling society to drive change.

The emergence of social design

Design, especially through iterations such as Service Design, has provided a fresh vehicle for designers, to legitimately and creatively enter into the backstage world of how all things are made and organised. Applying a design process to the arena of social change is the spectrum that this book is primarily concerned with.

Society driven design has been my practice for over two decades. The practice of collaborating with neighbourhoods and groups of people who drive their own change. In this sense, socially driven design cannot support the tastemaker element of design; the notion of a superhero designer telling a neighbourhood what 'good' looks like is flawed and simply doesn't work.

In seeking to define design and thus my relationship with my definition of design, I must accept a wider truth.
The only person I can change in this world is me, therefore neither myself or any other person operating in the arena of socially driven design can be *the* arbiter of *good*.

To collaborate well, and to encourage the skills that bring collective change means no designer has to infer what good looks like, as the collaborators must define good for themselves. When we collaborate, we are able to move closer towards Rousseau's collective understanding and objective. When we collaborate, *we* decide what *we* require.

In the mid 1860's John Ruskin wrote, "there is no wealth, but life[8] "- a life without the anxiety of being rejected because of nationality, a life with the freedom to engage without fear of exclusion, a life that guarantees a home for all. How can we accelerate towards a society where **all** can access that wealth? How can design ensure all are able to access that wealth? Design as a vehicle for social change was made explicit through Victor Papanek's 1970 landmark book,

---

[8] John Ruskin, Unto This Last, 1860, Cornhill Magazine Publications

Design for the Real World[9]. Papanek was encouraging designers to make things that met the needs of all people, not just the wants of some people, and in doing so, valuing the environment we live in. He citied the necessity for designers to be socially and morally responsible, thinking about the consequences of and manufacturing of their designs, taking into consideration the impact on the environment. Papanek urged designers to focus on needs, not wants and suggested the process for identifying these 'needs' should take place in heavily marginalised areas, where the designer should observe behaviour. There are themes that Papanek raises about the character of the designer that we will consider in the next chapter, however in the spirit of framing design, Papenk's book birthed the term social design. This iteration of design was seen as the deployment of values that were exercised in the making of physical things. In recent years social design can be defined as the application of design methodologies in order to tackle complex human issues. We are ever moving closer to Ruskin's maxim, and beyond Papenk's designing of physical objects, to explore the design of services, systems and indeed systems of systems.

As the scope of social design stretches its net further and further we are able to discern that socially driven design cannot solely live within the world of design methodologies, but must also incorporate an understanding of economic models, applied philosophy, political frameworks, the arts and entrepreneurship to name just a few.

When defining socially driven design we are not just defining design, but rather the approach that allows for all to have a stake in the process.

Design as a conversation
Design is an odd word; a noun, a verb and an adjective - and as such somewhat hard to define even outside of socially driven scenarios. When thinking of defining design should we be concerned with the aesthetic or about changing existing situations into preferred ones?

[9] Victor Papanek, Design for The Real World, 1971, Thames & Hudson, UK

More than exploring binary options, the word design might be used in social circles to demonstrate the height of sophistication, or a comprehensive term that covers all manner of design iterations, like the creation of clothing, interiors and cars. Perhaps for some, design simply means an intentional intervention, 'this has not happened by chance, no, this has occurred by design'. A product designer will no doubt provide a different definition of design than that of a fashion designer.

My personal definition of social design in the spirit of Papanek and Ruskin, is that of a conversation, one that takes place across space, time and culture. Defining design as a conversation is *my* definition of socially driven design, it is imperative that every designer defines their *own* understanding of design. As we will explore later in this movement, once we have defined design, the designer must then weave a compelling and honest relationship with it.

Embracing Papanek's definition of designing things that people need, we must believe that design can be applied at the most upstream intersections of our society as a means of seeking equitable collaborative change. We must also believe that for **all** to access the wealth of life that Ruskin speaks of, **all** must possess the basic tools by which to participate.

The designer must fashion their own definition of design in order to establish their own practice to support it.

Design, practiced as a conversation allows for all to participate in the collaborative process. This is an important factor as some iterations of design have unconsciously constructed a barrier between the designer and society. In more modern iterations of design, especially those approaches seeking to promote co-creation at its core, the continued employment of design jargon perpetuates the long standing impenetrable wall between designer and society.

A conversation however, allows for a far more universal threshold to be easily crossed, one where society is not required to conform to a post-it-note etiquette and more importantly, a process that is affirming of everyone. My work in prison, certainly at the genesis stage, would not have withstood any note-taking let alone traditional co-creation workshops with sharpies and post-it notes. I will expand more on this when sharing the InHouse Records story in the *beginnings* movement.

I spend the majority of my time, with people, in conversations. Not alone at a drawing table, or with other designers, clustered around a forest of laptops, but in conversation with people. The activities of the socially driven designer is that of crafting conversations where **all** feel confident to take part in. Making sense of the conversation and supporting the innovation that comes as a result of many conversations that all are able to take part in. The designer exploring society driven design will be spending most of their time making meaningful connections that enable all to participate.

When I began the long process of understanding the UK criminal justice system, the picture only began coming into focus when the conversations started. During that process I became strangely aware of my own insignificance; an overwhelming realisation that I was not the first person seeking to explore innovation across the criminal justice system. Many people have contributed far more than I. However, in seeking to understand their contributions, I was stretching a conversation across time and introducing a wider acknowledgement of all who had greatly contributed thus far. In choosing to see how countries like Norway or Japan approach justice, I was stretching the conversation across space and, by exploring how our societal rituals have formed and informed that which is around us, I was extending the conversation across culture. With each lengthening of the conversation, the stakeholder group grew, and by working hard to design fresh conversations regarding old stories, the engagement also rose. Design, in the application of societal change, can be a conversation across space, time and culture for all to participate in.

Conversations across space, time and culture

Language is a designed system for communication, and as such, an ancient design tool that everyone can access. With greater access comes greater participation, my practice has led me to believe that conversations can be the very process by which to understand, test and build initiatives of real change. All around us we can view multiple conversations taking place through the vehicle of trends, social norms and local customs. Sometimes these conversations are unconscious, further reinforcing my belief that for socially driven change, design is a conversation, across space, time and culture.

Miles Davis performing, *Someday My Prince Will Come*[10] the title track of his 1961 album, is a conversation across space, time and culture. Walt Disney, who originally featured the same track sung by Adriana Caselotti in the 1937 hand drawn animation of, *Snow White*[11] began the dialogue. A conversation between Davis and Caselotti, but also between the audiences of jazz music and Disney cartoons, from children with their families, travelling to cinemas, to adults listening to live music in clubs or purchasing vinyl to playback on their record players. By including two very different demographics, this conversation was able to reach a much wider section of society.

When Max Richter remixed Vivaldi on his breathtaking project *Recomposed*[12], he wasn't remixing an audio recording of Vivaldi's *Four Seasons*, as there was no way of making a master recording of Vivaldi's music in 1720, instead Richter embarked upon a task of literally re-mixing Vivaldi's notes on paper. The result is an incredible conversation spanning almost three hundred years, from 1720 to 2014. Back in 1720, only those who held privilege places in society were able to enjoy access to Vivaldi's music and they were only able to listen to the music if it was being played live. Richter's album, *Recomposed*, is not restricted to commissioned recitals for the socially elite but available to anyone who has a digital device and, whilst streaming is

---

[10] Miles Davis, Someday My Prince Will Come, 1961, Colombia Records

[11] Snow White and The Seven Dwarfs, 1937, Disney Pictures

[12] Max Richter, Recomposed Vivaldi Four Seasons, 2012, Universal Music

still exclusive to those that can access data, the re-creation of *Recomposed* is far more equitable than that of Vivaldi's time.

A conversation, across space, time and culture for all.

When Christopher Nolan imagined the cinematic event of Batman's, *Dark Knight* trilogy[13] he demonstrated a deep respect of the graphic novels by Frank Miller; *Batman Year One*[14] and the *Dark Knight Returns*.[15] In this conversation across space, time and culture, Nolan shares the same story through a different medium, from comic strip to frames of a film and in doing so, exponentially grew the participants of this superhero conversation.

Conversations defining design
Conversations that are progressive across time, will often have an iterative nature to them. Conversations can be adaptive in their learning.

When we change one part of a conversation, everything is changed, if only marginally. Ezio Manzini[16], explains the changing nature of services by bringing them closer to people. Communities that can access face to face services within ten minutes walk of their neighbourhood. Corner shops hosting council representatives, unused spaces can become surgeries or advice centres. Changing the conversation through proximity.

The excellent work currently being undertaken by Thomas Horton overseeing Grand Avenues, brings the practice of probation closer to people who are on probation and in doing so, changes the quality of the probation experience. Moving the conversation away from the probation office and into the neighbourhoods changes the experience for probation officer and the person on probation.

---

13 Christopher Nolan, Dark Knight Trilogy, 2005-2012, Warner Bros

14 Frank Miller, Batman Year One, 1987, DC Comics

15 Frank Miller, Dark Knight Returns, 1986, DC Comics

16 Ezio Manzini, Design When Everybody Wins, 2015, MIT Press

Manet, Music in the Tuileries, 1862.

Manet, The Railway, 1873.

Proximity changes the quality of the service. Grand Avenues encourages meaningful engagement, more transparency, greater honesty and deeper trust.

Changing the conversation through proximity in these example makes the service different - yet still the same - closer and more accessible. Nolan's Batman is the same, but more accessible to a wider section of society. Richter brought Vivaldi to people who had never experienced classical music. It is the same, but different, closer, more accessible. Beautifully crafted conversations have the power to illuminate and make ideas attainable.

Edouard Manet is considered one of the founding fathers of Modernism and in doing so, he bridged the gap between realism and impressionism. With Manet I always feel his deeper message is somewhere on the edge of the canvas or sometimes it's not on the canvas at all. He used his practice to communicate beauty, hope, social awareness and inequality. Charles Dickens was adept at bringing issues that society found unpalatable, into the mainstream through his brilliant storytelling. Indeed, he did more than just bring work houses and orphans to the public consciousness, he challenged the layered status of class by constantly melting it all through his stories. With Dickens, social status was not an indicator of kindness neither was being a gentleman - often in his stories the kindest person does not belong to the social elite - this in of itself was shocking for readers at the time. Manet, would do the same through his brilliant draughtsmanship skills. Often painting the everyday scenes of Paris, but at a scale only reserved for iconic religious images, which caused scandal because Manet made the everyday sacred. Using the mediums of literature and art, both Manet and Dickens were creating conversations across space, time and culture, conversations that provoked society into further discussion.

In the year 1862 Manet painted, *Music in the Tuileries*[17]. When viewing the painting the observer is presented with a crowded scene but senses there is something not quite right.

---

[17] Edouard Manet, Music in the Tuileries, 1862

The painting is named *Music in the Tuileries*, and yet we cannot see any musicians or musical instruments. By a gradual process of elimination the viewer begins to realise that may be they are the musicians, elevated to the stage of performance.

Manet chose to paint his friends, collaborators and peers as his subject, and at such a large scale, traditionally reserved only for religious icons or past masters and thus, in doing so, offended many exhibition goers. This is because they perceived Manet to be exalting himself and his social circle to that of a higher status. However - and I am stressed to point out - I have no insight into Manet's thoughts, I see a collaborative spirit in Manet, who was choosing to portray all the people that are part of assembling and applying his practice, and this included his audience too. Manet demonstrated an inseparable quality between the artist and the audience.

If design is a conversation, then the conversation should be for all. If the conversation is about prisons, for example, then judges, prison officers, prisoners and police need to be part of the conversation, as much as other stakeholders. All who are part of the conversation, must stay in the conversation long after the initiatives are made, their involvement in the conversation shouldn't be merely for extractive research or interviews but a commitment to make something together or perhaps many things? All must be in the conversation if we seek societal change, in the same way that all are featured in Manet's *Tuileries garden*.

Defining Design - to what end?
In 1873, eleven years after *Music at the Tuileries*, Manet painted *The Railway*[18]. Typical of Manet, there is no actual railway to be clearly identified and the painting is fuelled with enormous ambiguity. Manet captures the societal concerns of Paris, a city anxious to know what impact the second industrial revolution will have on everyday lives. Manet depicts the fear and anxiety that many were feeling towards technology and what this technology may have meant as nineteenth

_____

[18] Edouard Manet, The Railway, 1873

century society firmly embraced the throes of change. Manet's response to all this social anxiety was to provide the space for ambiguity. In the painting we are presented with characters whose connection to each other is vague and ambiguous. We are not sure how the woman is connected to the little girl, if at all and just to add further obscurity, we cannot see the face of the girl. However even more vague is the railway hidden by a cloud of steam. Perhaps this is the point that Manet was hoping to make: the future is unknown, and even he didn't want to imagine it.

Every designer must define their own understanding of design, and in doing so, will dictate what they actually design. Therefore it is essential to go beyond the definition of the design, by asking of oneself 'to what end?'

This first movement has been written specifically to encourage the designer on an internal journey, to define design, to define the subsequent relationship towards design and how that definition equips our vocabulary to speak of endings. To what end am I designing conversations across space, time and culture? This internal question led me to a realisation that I can only truly change one person, myself. I cannot change anyone else, at best I can hope to positively contribute to the lives of others.

In the spirit of Manet's railway, I cannot presume to change the future, but I can contribute to making the space for a collaborative change to take place. Therefore, it is my belief that the goal of the socially driven designer should be to create the *space* for change to take place, not the change itself. Allowing those who are collaborating, through conversations, to be the architects of their own change.

Design is a conversation across space, time and culture. A conversation for all; in order to establish truth, enabling the conditions for purposeful collaboration and the space for change to take place.

Endings Part Two
Relationship with Design

I think you may be surprised by your own definitions of design, especially for those choosing to define design for social change.

In this second chapter we will explore the relationship that the designer needs to construct with their newly defined version of design. The relationship between design and the designer can also be called 'a practice' and over the next few pages we will be examining how to build and maintain a practice. Defining design requires us to describe our relationship with design, and in order to do that we must have an understanding of who we are.

My practice protects the principles for conversations across space, time and culture - with everyone - establishing the conditions for change to emerge. My practice is the most portable application of my role as a designer, it provides an indication of who I am to others, and offers a North Star by which I seek to chart my vocation.

The designer, is defined internally, by their values, beliefs and understanding. A practice permits one to know themselves and to be known. To be true to themselves at all times. These internal qualities are often tacit and may fully or in part remain hidden. Only when our practice can be articulated do we have a chance of improving, personally and professionally. If we cannot see what we know, how are we to advance our craft?

As designers who are keen to see a better way of being human, we must give everything. This requires us to be explicit regarding our aspirations; values, beliefs, and societal frameworks.

Our values drive our behaviour. We act in certain ways because we think in certain ways. Values that are important to us are afforded an elevated hierarchy than those we deem less worthy.

Our values can often go unchecked, so if we do not articulate our practice, we are in effect outsourcing tacit decisions regarding our own life. Giving the rights to understand ourselves away without ever being aware they were ours in the first place. For the designer, to articulate their values is to win back agency, providing the opportunity for improvement.

Articulating our own values may feel challenging, however, without doing so, improvement becomes impossible.

Once we are cognisant of our values we can add aspiration. The process of making the invisible, visible, allows us to choose not just the kind of designer we wish to be, but the kind of human we desire to be. How we behave is often tempered by our past experiences, but defining how we wish to behave can be a liberating experience.

In 1882 - considered to be his last major work - Manet painted, *A bar at the Folies-Bergère*[19]. There is nothing I can add of any merit to the critical art historians understanding of this painting, but I can share my personal relationship with, *A bar at the Folies-Bergère*. When looking at the painting I am presented with a scene, the immediacy of a moment, like joining a conversation that is already in progress. I view this painting regularly, visiting the Courtlands Gallery, off the Strand in London and will always find myself staring at the canvas, lost in an altogether different world. I imagine I have just been asked by the girl behind the bar 'what would you like to drink?' She is staring back at me, waiting for my response. I can barely hear myself think perhaps all of Paris is in attendance tonight. My eyes are drawn to the Champagne but the activity in the mirror behind her is distracting me. Retuning to her stare, I fear she is growing impatient, waiting for my order, 'wait, what is that?' The legs of a trapeze artist in the mirror, I turn around to marvel at the sight of a lady swinging from cords fixed to the ceiling.

---

[19] Edouard Manet, A bar at the Folies-Bergère, 1882

Manet, A bar at the Folies-Bergère, 1882.

'Monsieur?' I rotate to face the barmaid once more, her stoic demeanour is weighing on me. I should order, there are patrons behind me wishing to quench their thirst. I decide on Champagne, yet before I can utter the words, I catch a glimpse of someone in the mirror. Me. What happens when we look in the mirror and we do not recognise the face that is starring back at us?

I have no idea what Manet wanted his audiences to think when standing in front of the *Bar at the Folies-Bergère* painting, however the central placing of the barmaid meant that anyone who stood staring at the picture, could view an alternative image of themselves. With Manet, the message is rarely on the canvas and, perhaps he wanted the world to know that his picture would only be complete if someone stood in front of it. *A bar at the Folies-Bergère* is my constant refresh and starting point for my practice. I go to view it, to remind myself who I want to be, and the change I want to be part of. By extensions, and as a means of developing the designers practice, I have highlighted a series of values for the reader to grapple with, test and perhaps, apply across their own practice. In effect, I am sharing with you what I feel when I stare at Manet's *bar at the Folies-Bergère.*

Truth
Truth is a personal response and founding principle to building my relationship with design. If design is a conversation across space, time and culture, then not only must I request truth from those taking part in order to build conversations that are real, I must also demand truth of myself. If we are aspiring to access truth or speak truth into conversations, then we must first ensure we are able to be true to ourselves.

I am reminded of Polonius' speech from Shakespeare's Hamlet:

"This above all: to thine own self be true, and it must follow, as the night the day, thou cans't not then be false to any man.[20]" If the designer is true to their self, then it naturally follows that they will be

---

[20] William Shakespeare, Hamlet, 2021, Independently Published, UK

true to others as well. However the negative is also true, in *The Quintessence of Ibsenism*, for instance, George Bernard Shaw wrote: "the liar's punishment is, not in the least that he is not believed, but that he cannot believe any one else.[21]"

Honest behaviour is important not just because dishonest behaviour harms other people, but possibly more importantly, because dishonest behaviour ultimately harms oneself, as one becomes convinced that the rest of the world is as unfaithful as they are. Shakespeare crystallises this theme in his play *Othello*[22], whereby the leading character, Othello, murders his wife, Desdemona, because he has been convinced of her unfaithfulness - inventing examples of evidence to *prove* infidelity. Dishonest behaviour distorts our perception of others, and subsequently our perception of the world.

Fusing Socrates and Shakespeare as a maxim for designers seeking to drive change by society: "Know thy self, and to thine own self be true."

The designer should be encouraged to speak their elected truth, speaking into what 'can be' as well as what 'already is.' We must show better ways of being, whether that's a better building, a better product, a better garment, or a better service; the designer must encourage us all to do life better.

This is the truth of creativity that Ruskin is urging us to grasp: "if you are not speaking truth you are using creativity in a wasteful manner.[23]" It is a bold ask of us, but then again, for all who are committed to seeing a better world, this is a truth we should have all already adopted. The mirror in the *Bar at the Folies-Bergère* provides a primary checkpoint for our internal design journey. The mirror can reveal who we are and who we want to become. What happens if we look in the

---

21 George Bernard Shaw, The Quintessence of Ibsenism, 1891, Dover Publications, UK

22 William Shakespeare, Othello, 2000, Penguin, UK

23 John Ruskin, Modern Painters Volume One, 1843, John Wiley and Sons

mirror and do not like what we see? As designers who wish to engage in positively contributing to social change, the mirror at *A bar at the Folies-Bergère* is where we can prepare for our own change.

Reflection

Engaging with the mirror at Folies-Bergère, requires the activity of reflection. Carving out the time and space to become better known to ourselves, a conversation with ourselves across time. The value of reflection is that it provides an opportunity to view our behaviour through different lenses and encourages the activity of personal change. Society is changing constantly, so we too must adapt if we seek positive change in our society.

Reflection as improvement is not a new practice, indeed many of us are well versed with the medium of smart watches, feeding us health data that provide new routines for improvement, but what would a watch that supplies data on our behaviour look like? What would a watch that dispenses data on our thoughts look like? The practice of reflection, is to capture exactly those behavioural insights in order to establish a pathway for improvement.

How do we maintain a good relationship between ourselves, the designer, and design if we do not reflect? Reflection permits the designer to choose who they desire to become or whom they no longer wish be. The need for the designer to internally incorporate truth and reflection will open a rich vein that can be dedicated to improvement.

The concepts of accurate research and detailed user journeys are familiar ones to many designers, however when exploring our ultimate user journey from birth to death, the internal research we conduct of ourselves becomes critical not only to our improvement, but to the improvement of the lives around us.

Rumi, the mid 13th century Persian poet wrote: "our goal, as human beings, is to understand ourselves better and become more grateful, resilient, confident and productive in our daily life.[24]" As people who wish to contribute to improving society, we should not only be open to improving ourselves, but actively seeking to do so.

The mirror at Folies-Bergère reveals what is hidden from others. Reflecting back to me the razor cuts of an anxious morning, or the best mask of a smile I can conjure to conceal a heavy heart. The mirror is the place where we are able to be honest with ourselves and each other. The mirror is the place where we can focus on how we may wish to incorporate change in our own lives. Truth between myself and the design process I am speaking into. The truth of the exploded drawing, revealing the complex components, the truth of the supply chains that disclose the conditions of the garment factory. Society driven design requires the designer to host conversations of truth.

The author Richard Sennett, writes beautifully about the attributes of the craftsman[25]. On the subject of truth both he and Ruskin agree that the human who seeks to make things, must first make sure they themselves are ready to be changed and open to change in their own life. The designer seeking to contribute to social change, must accept the first material they have access to shape is themselves and thus, ensure there is an honest adaptability to that material.

The designer must seek their own mirrors, providing opportunities for honest reflection, that can cultivate development.

I have sought many 'mirrors' in my life to ensure the space for reflection and I would encourage the socially driven designer to do

---

[24] Rumi, Little Book Of Life, 2019 Harper Collins, UK

[25] Richard Sennett, The Craftsman, 2008, Yale University Press, USA

likewise. Crucially, it is important to weave this into a regular routine, once a week write down characteristics that you wish to amplify or ones you wish to eliminate. You may already have your own reflective practices, however if not, I would suggest you employ something that can provide the scope to regularly investigate yourself.

Knowing ourselves reveals our motivations, the designer can leverage these for articulating truth.

Invisible Sacrifices

Making anything will always demand a sacrifice from the maker. There exists a socio- economic principle, namely, to make anything we must first be prepared to give something up (sometimes we must give up more than just one thing).

Ruskin was far more interested in that which the designer was willing to sacrifice than what the designer was going to make. As makers, we should have a clear understanding of what we are willing to sacrifice, as well as viewing the act of creation as a sacrifice itself. The time we give, for instance, is a sacrifice, and in terms of social impact, there will be plenty of occasions where our time will not be rewarded or acknowledged at all.

I choose to sacrifice time, a decade per phenomena. This is a sacrifice of time, in order to better understand the language of the phenomena. After a decade in homelessness, I was able to become more fluent in the diverse languages that different stakeholders communicated through and thus, I was more sufficiently equipped to host conversations for all to access, across space time and culture. Similarly after almost a decade of exploring the criminal justice system, I am able to host conversations with far more clarity, presenting wider scope for change to take place.

My desire to operate in decades is a sacrifice that I hope will deliver outcomes that support positive impact. However it is a risk, my time in homelessness delivered less impact than I had wanted. As you choose the aspirational values that define you as a designer, be sure to explore the boundaries of what sacrifice might look like for you.

Sacrifices are not merely what we choose to give up, but can also be what we choose to hide. These are often called invisible sacrifices and historically have alluded to craftsmen making things of real beauty that no one will ever see. A church of gothic architecture; tall with pointy arches, a ribbed vaulted ceiling and flying buttresses all convey the grandeur of a magnificent building. A cluster of columns are located within the church, one side visible, and one side hidden against the interior wall. Many gothic craftsman would still sculpt the detail of the vine or the sprout of the leaf at the top of the column, knowing it would be impossible for the public to view. Their craft embraced the value of an invisible sacrifice.

To carefully weave beauty and excellence that will be hidden into the work; invisible sacrifices, offer the opportunity for craft, making something known only to the designer. For many this remains an important value of making things, embedding invisible sacrifices, helping to ensure a high standard of quality is always present.

In PT Anderson's period drama, *Phantom Thread*,[26] Daniel Day-Lewis plays a high-end dressmaker, who designs sought after gowns for royalty and the upper echelons of society. In the film his character weaves unique hidden messages into the canvas of all his customers' garments, messages known only to him. This kind of invisible sacrifice can be implicit in the designs we are all working towards. What might an invisible sacrifice look like in the work you are involved in? Would you feature invisible sacrifices as part of an aspirational value set within your own practice?

Many believe these invisible sacrifices should be known only to the maker, by doing so, they retain greater significance and validate the sacrifice of the maker. However you choose to navigate your understanding and maybe even your application of invisible sacrifices, remember that the greater purpose of sacrifices are to enrich improvement, as a designer and as a human.

---

[26] PT Anderson, Phantom Thread, 2017, Universal Pictures

Visible Sacrifices

As well as exploring the value of hiding our sacrifices, it is important that we are also aware of the sacrifices we choose to make known. An elite athlete, for example, will sacrifice much to perform at the height of their ability; ensuring diet, sleep, training and mental wellbeing are all considered in a bid to serve with excellence in their chosen field of sport. This should also be the case for the society driven designer, and the sacrifices afforded for working in the area of social impact; ensuring that we are able to offer excellence in craft and thought. For many, the pursuit of craft may take on a more monastic or spiritual narrative that affects how we live and, whilst that may be too extreme for some, it is worth examining what are the conditions needed to operate at a higher than optimal standard. What might it look like if a designer was in training for social impact?

All change requires sacrifice.

To achieve change we must understand our starting position and then define where it is that we are heading towards. I have spoken at length regarding the articulation our values, this enables us to locate *where* we are.

The mirror at Folies-Bergère, becomes a lens by which to understand the self. However the people that surround us, like those at the Tuileries, can also become mirrors who reflect back to us what they see. Through a range of different mirrors we can identify where we are and, what we need to sacrifice in order to change.

Our labour, could be seen as the most precious material we are contributing to the design process. Labour is a sacrifice and therefore becomes an opportunity to challenge ourselves in always giving our best. It's not the gold leaf or the Italian marble, nor is it the latest MacBook Pro; it is not the tools nor the materials, but our time that is the most beautiful offering we can bring to all that we make. If we view our labour as a beautiful sacrifice, then we will surely want to make our contribution the best it can be.

...adise is Here 2014 - 2019
...missioned by the Guild of St. George

There
is no
wealth
but
life

We live in a time where the prevalent approaches to work appear to be productivity and efficiency; producing the best results within the least amount of time. For those exploring the world of social impact we may wish to investigate alternative approaches for valuing how we get things done; treating everything as a cost saving exercise may yield financially sound initiatives, but what of the actual impact? What do we need to sacrifice in order to achieve a different set of outcomes?

The designer must sacrifice something in order to make anything. Visible and invisible sacrifices will often define the quality of what we 'make', and indeed what we make of ourselves.

Gratitude
Gratitude has been the passport to my personal change. It took me many difficult years to value what I have, instead of yearning for what I have not. Perhaps a lack of gratitude supports the foundation of a deficit model and perhaps, the presence of gratitude forms the understructure of an asset based approach? By focusing on what's strong, not what's wrong, we are not just choosing to see the strengths that we possess, but also learning to truly value all we have.

I am grateful for all I have, the air that I breathe, the life I am privileged to live, the part of the world I am rooted in, the communities and networks that nourish me. I am grateful for every moment of my life. This gratitude helps me to see beyond myself, to see my insignificance; and in the process appreciate all that surrounds me.

By practicing gratitude, I am able to better acknowledge the goodness that takes shape across my life. If this is a foreign concept to you, then I would strongly recommend the incorporation of gratitude on a daily basis. Gratitude helps us engage with positive emotions, relish good experiences, improve our mental health, deal with adversity and build strong relationships. In design, gratitude plays a significant role as it empowers us to honour that which we already have, before we seek to improve.

The art of gratitude facilitates conversations across space, time and culture. My desire, for socially driven design, is to establish the conditions for change to take place, when gratitude is practiced inclusion becomes greater and deeper and the potential for change to occur increases exponentially.

Humility

One of Aristotle's twelve virtues: humility, is the quality or state of not thinking you are better than others. The leap from gratitude to humility is a symbiotic one, more of one, increases the other. With greater gratitude comes greater humility, and vice versa.

Humility is a building block of collaboration and without this virtue, any collaborative design attempt may descend into unhealthy reinforcements of existing de-centred power dynamics. My greatest significance in life is realising how insignificant I am. This isn't a repeated mock modesty mantra, but a realisation that can liberate the mind of a designer. By respecting every human, and bowing before everyone, (metaphorically or literally) we are recognising the humanity in us all. It is through humility that we are able to hear other people's voices and through humility that we are able to listen to alternative opinions.

Rumi, once wrote: "The whole universe is contained within a single human being - you.[27]" It is humility that provides us with the freedom to collaborate, believing that others have unique and significant contributions. Humility is a design value that provides the building block for collaboration.

However humility provides more than just a gateway to making alliances, it graces us with the ability to say no. The designer needs humility to reject projects where the risk of causing more harm than good is present. Every society driven designer must be humble enough to acknowledge first of all, we must do no harm.

---

[27] Rumi, Essential Rumi, 1995, Penguin, UK

Humility, not just to decide if the work should be undertaken or not, (which should be an evergreen consideration), but also if we are the right person to undertake the work at all? Humility empowers us to see other designers who may be better equipped than us, and it is humility that imparts the grace to suggest other designers undertake work that had been originally offered to us.

Honesty and Kindness

Honesty, is at the heart of all healthy relationships, starting with the inner relationship that we all have with ourselves as well as the relationships we share with others. If I am unable to be honest with myself, I stand very little chance of contributing to sustainable change for others.

Honesty to deliver unpopular news, or honesty to provide frank appraisals can still be delivered with kindness, but kindness without honesty becomes a dangerous precedent to set.

In our lives the practice of kindness provides scope for connection. There is real beauty when something has been designed, in a manner that encourages people to be kinder to each other. I am reminded of Charles Dickens, whom throughout all of his work deployed two common themes; do not judge people and be kind to each other. He used the social framework of class to show how we are biased to judge, and in doing so we miss the acts of kindness that are taking place. In almost every story, Dickens created at least one character that sought to inspire the reader to survey better ways of being human.

After the release of Dickens' *A Christmas Carol,*[28] the novelist William Thackeray wrote a heartfelt review in Fraser's Magazine saying: "It seems to me a national benefit, and to every man or woman who reads it a personal kindness.[29]"

---

[28] Charles Dickens, A Christmas Carol, 2003, Penguin, UK

[29] https://www.charlesdickenspage.com/charles-dickens-a-christmas-carol.html#:~:text=William Makepeace Thackeray in Fraser's,'"

Incredibly Dickens originally self published the novel as he was unable to receive the backing from any publishing company. The book has never been out of print since its publication in 1843. Incidentally soon after the release of the book public donations soared, a book that evokes national kindness.

Honesty and kindness in our practice are essential for those we are collaborating with, as we are also mirrors that reflect behaviour - and if we are unable to be true and kind, then we are in danger of reflecting back values that may cause division. Our role, as those wanting to affect change in our society, is to form a healthy and kind relationship with honesty, to be brave enough to reveal aspects of our initiatives that may have previously remained hidden for the wrong reasons and creative enough to rebalance.

Our practice, first and foremost becomes a crucible for personal change. "I must change!" wrote Rumi. "Yesterday I was clever, so I wanted to change the world. Today I am wise, so I am changing myself.[30]"

I might be wrong in my thinking and in view of this I hold my opinions lightly. There is something beautiful about integrating failure in a holistic way or directly hard-wiring failure into my practice. There is also something intoxicating about being ready to let go of long held thoughts, if I can see a kinder way or better still, if someone else can demonstrate a kinder way then I will embrace it wholeheartedly.

A designer must know themselves, in order to know what they must sacrifice, and be true to themselves at all times, in order to understand that which they must change.

[30] Rumi, Essential Rumi, 1995, Penguin, UK

Compassion

Compassion, means *to suffer together* and amongst emotional intelligence researchers, compassion is defined as the feeling that arises when someone is confronted with another's suffering and as a result feels motivated to relieve that suffering.

However, before we may be able to demonstrate compassion we must first demonstrate empathy. Without empathy we may be in danger of not really understanding the viewpoint of other person or their needs. Empathy helps us - like humility - to hear the voice of those who are rarely given a platform to speak and, to understand their journey. It is empathy that helps us stop and observe. By listening to someone else's suffering, we become aware of the feelings arising to relieve that pain. Empathy focuses our emotions; thus providing a vehicle to access compassion by demonstrating acts of kindness.

Sympathy may well be the result of an individual feeling sorry for another, or perhaps imagining what another persons suffering might be like, however empathy drives us to connect with people and find out from those experiencing the difficulty to understand what they are actually 'going-though'. Compassion helps us move away from competing with one another toward collaboration with each other, allowing us to view human beings, not as different but the same; fellow travellers to the grave (and perhaps beyond).

Empathy and compassion will often drive us, as humans and designers, to acts of kindness born from generosity. Generosity can be the giving away of that which we have an abundance of, this does not have to be money - and in some cases money may not be the right thing to give regardless. Generosity of time, generosity of thought and generosity of care for example are accessible to most.

The designer connects with people through empathy; understanding someone else's situation by asking, not assuming. Connecting through empathy, acting through compassion.

As designers who are empathetic, compassionate, kind and generous, we will begin to find ourselves accepted in communities, neighbourhoods, tribes and collectives. Indeed, this is precisely where we should be, if we wish to see society drive design and create the conditions for change. We must be precisely where Papanek suggested we travel to, the places that design rarely goes to.

Thus far we have discussed values and attributes that can support the designer in forging strong relationships between themselves and the definition of design. These values, aspirations and attributes form part of the designers practice. However, I am minded to share how our values can be applied to an approach that can serve to ensure socially driven design retains a high standard of detail and care. In order to achieve this, we will be exploring the art of craftsmanship as the key vehicle for the designer to establish a positive relationship with design itself.

Whilst I have never known how to solve other people's problems, nor would I want to, I am passionate about providing the safe and enabling environments for individuals to solve their own problems. When people solve their own problems, they often do so by creating their own change and building their own capacity for future challenges which they may face. Providing safe and enabling environments where collaboration and learning become the heartbeat of a functioning and thriving neighbourhood. I started my design practice because I believe that real transformation and reconciliation occur when done *with and by* others who are equally as hungry for change in their lives, as I am in my own.

Craftsmanship Between the Designer and Design
Craftsmanship may be understood as the level of skill a craftsman possesses. A master craftsman would be expected to make crafts of the finest quality. What drives a craftsman is their motivation.

In his profound book, *The Craftsman*[31], Richard Sennett, states rather unambiguously that motivation is superior to skill. Sennet is drawing our attention to the importance of why we make things.

By making things well, we develop techniques that enable us to improve and the desire to make things well is sometimes called a craft. Making things well is a capacity all humans possess but it is seldom honoured in today's society. The craft of parenting, choosing to approach the life long activity of nurturing life is rarely recognised as a craft.

We all experience building relationships, sustaining them, iterating and sometimes ending them. Doing all these stages well, and indeed improving on each of these stages, could be seen as taking the art of relationships seriously enough to view it as a craft. Of course in both cases of parenting and relationships, the motivation is key to the quality of improvement.

Craftsmanship *can* occur within anything we spend considerable time making. For craftsmanship to occur depends on whether we care to improve the process and quality of that which we are making.

Maybe you have experienced the satisfaction of making something and then experienced even greater satisfaction of making the same thing but better than before. This sense of wellbeing provides more than just a good feeling, it becomes the space for us to think clearly, identifying approaches to certain challenges and the environment for self improvement. As designers, our craft helps us become better at becoming better, and craftsmanship helps us to make better contributions. Without craftsmanship, our work creates a means-to-ends thinking and we become instruments in the process. It becomes problematic if the things we make regularly are detached of craft; for example, if we make things without wanting to get better at making them, both the craft and the maker became detached of meaning.

---

[31] Richard Sennett, The Craftsman, 2008, Yale University Press, USA

Ezio Manzini, speaks of: "making things well, not disabling wellbeing [32]". Throughout history we have made things better, when we have made them together.

Guilds were spaces where like minded communities would gather to make things, make them exceptionally well and by default become crucibles for improvement. The quality for Guilds to deliver craft training - and as a by-product personal improvement - became so famed, that parents would entrust the education of their children to the Guilds. Evidence for the existence of Guilds date back to 2200BC in Assyria and Mesopotamia, however in Europe our modern understanding of Guilds has been informed by the Romans, and throughout the Middle Ages across Europe.

To achieve this harmony of craft, quality artefacts and personal improvement, Guilds required excellent social organisation, in the pursuit of craftsmanship - making things well. In comparison today we may identify poorly organised institutions, as places where there is no goal to make anything, but purely to solve problems per se. One could argue that the craft for such organisations is that of making solutions, however this can be challenging if not properly married with problem finding, value finding, teamwork and collaboration. The social organisation of the Guilds served as a contributor to craft. Modern institutions seldom demonstrate the harmony of making things well, personal improvement and societal education.

The Guilds required the presence of the whole person to make something and thus, the Guild as an organisation could make many things to an exceptional standard due to the motivation of the craftsmen. When motivation is extracted and thus the opportunity for someone to improve on what they are making is removed, we resort to means-to-ends thinking, which often results in us not needing to engage our whole minds in carrying out our jobs, and so our minds are prone to wander.

[32] Ezio Manzini, Design When Everybody Wins, 2015, MIT Press

HOLDING A CONVERSATION WITH ANOTHER PERSON IS TO ENGAGE IN A HIGHLY CREATIVE PROCESS.

"An adult, speaker, who has somehow acquired an amazing range of abilities, which enable him in particular to say what he means, to understand what people say to him, to do this in a fashion that I think is proper to call highly creative."

Chomsky 1971

Aspects of the service industry can be a example of this, the employee at the checkout till may be physically there, but then again they may have checked out weeks ago due to the lack of engagement as the boredom of their work becomes unbearable. The mortgage advisor could be going through the motions to customers on one side of the table and yet rapidly updating their social media profile as they seek to find ways of injecting meaning into their work.

There are many other sectors besides the service industry that allow for multi-tasking, lulling employees into a false sense of security, that jobs are done by simply turning up and being passive. Services need to be crafted, ensuring those who are benefiting from the service are able to experience it as beautifully as those who are delivering the service. The craft in designing services, should have the scope to support all staff, not just those delivering, but those supporting those who are delivering through the creation of resources and tools to do so sustainably, informatively and pro-actively.

In his bestselling book, *Small is Beautiful*, E.F Schumacher wrote: "Mans needs are infinite but materialism is finite. Infinite comes only from spirituality.[33]" When we make things together we are also learning. When the motivation to make things well is hard-wired through the social organisation, our needs are being more sustainably met. Part of the designers remit is to make things with enough resistance to inspire curiosity.

The Guilds, through an organisational structure that promoted 'making as learning', advanced growth in deep rooted ways. Two important themes that emerged were curiosity and repetition. We can see these themes prevalent in modern society, but they are no longer in the form of Guilds, but seen in the ubiquity and often isolated phenomena of gaming.

---

[33] E.F Schumacher, Small is Beautiful, 1973, Vintage

The designed environment of the Guilds is that of *doing not telling*, promoting concentration through being present. In such an environment we are able to make things well, as well as make things intuitively. Collaboration births creativity that is collective and in an altogether different meaning than that of Rouseau's social contract, the collective intuition evolves from designing socially together.[34]

It's this collective intuition that Ruskin calls the "lamp of power[35]." Something that stirs inside us all but we are unable to describe. Ruskin encourages craftsmen to make things that are not merely liked because they are understood, but to make things that are liked without being understood. This level of excellence and craftsmanship is a direct product of society driven design; to make something and to make it so well, that it is valued without being able to be fully explained. The embodied knowledge of the collaborators becomes inherent in the design, like social DNA.

This level of craftsmanship can be implicit in the work being carried out, or it can be in choices that are made, choices that have been predetermined by constraints.

Victor Papanek, would argue that humans have forgotten that we have been designed 'to do', not just to consume and we should move from mass production to production by the masses. This requires the ability to socially organise the spaces for work and requires society to drive these initiatives, in a similar fashion to the evolution of the Guilds themselves.

Ezio Manzini reminds us that much as we are marvelling at our own ingenuity in technological advancements that are seeking to increase convenience, we are rapidly becoming more de-skilled in the process,

34 Jean-Jacques Rousseau, The Social Contract, 1762

35 John Ruskin, The Seven Lamps of Architecture, 1989 Dover Publications, UK

echoing Sennett's remarks that "doing things well is seldom honoured in our modern society[36]."

Since growing up in the 1970's, I have gradually seen in many sectors, a de-skilling of society, as services and products have liberated us from many onerous everyday chores and increased efficiency within the workplace, (or the appearance of efficiency); this has allowed for certain aspects of our lives to become easier - but in the process, and as an unconscious by-product - we have become more independent and less collaborative. Manzini calls this a state of disabling wellbeing[37].

As an immigrant to the United Kingdom, I had to forge my own pathway into belonging, and during the process, I had to learn new skills that invited collaboration and stimulated interdependence, a virtuous process of enabling wellbeing. The phenomena of *belonging* to a place where you find yourself an outsider is a repetitive one. Starting afresh every day, needing to demonstrate a daily social agility, just to belong, and re-belong, and re-belong again. The equivalent of building oneself from scratch everyday for many, many days on end. Integration can be exhaustive.

Making things, and doing them well, reminds us we are human. Ruskin returns to the theme of craft in *Seven Lamps of Architecture[38]* when he shares that the human spirit of making something beautiful, something pleasing or elegant to engage with is a sprit we all possess.

William Morris wasn't just a pioneer for the Arts & Crafts movement, he was also a pioneer for the craftsman in us all, to be freed. He saw that society was losing the ability to make things 'together' and make them well. He saw the diminishing attribute of craftsmanship rapidly

----

[36] Richard Sennett, Together, 2012, Penguin, UK

[37] Ezio Manzini, Design When Everybody Wins, 2015, MIT Press

[38] John Ruskin, The Seven Lamps of Architecture, 1989 Dover Publications, UK

affecting a generation. Morris & Co inspired a movement, to make things. Somewhere along the line we have forgotten to make things together, with honestly, kindness and compassion. Modern society has hollowed out the craftsman from us all.

Endings Part Three
The Language of Endings

"Attention must be paid!"
A line from Arthur Miller's play, *Death of a Salesman.*[39] The excerpt is taken from a passionate speech given by Willy Lomans' wife, Linda Loman, who is choosing to see beyond the deceptions and self deceptions of her husband, in favour of seeing the man.

Willy Loman is portrayed in Miller's play, as a twisted, anfractuous man, who found the skills of a salesman to be inadequate for meaningful relationships. Researchers estimate the average person in the UK is exposed to ten thousand adverts per day. What happens to our soul when we are exposed to the constant radiation fallout of consumerism and capitalism? For Willy Loman he was unable to escape the grip of his crippling self comparison with a tragically imperfect pursuit of status.

What happens to us when we are consistently bombarded with sales? The meta narrative of being regularly presented with 'new' diminishes our ability to emotionally and cognitively reflect on endings.

From new products, to new jobs, from *this* season's fashion offerings to the latest subscription based dating app, we are awash with the promise of 'new' but who will speak of endings? Design has to play its part in fabricating the conversational forum on how things can end and

---

39 Arthur Miller, Death of a Salesman, 2022, Methuen Drama; 1st edition, UK

how things can end well. We should be apportioning as much time towards the craft of designing better endings, as we do the inordinate amount of resources that are deployed to selling 'new'.

Articulating the Internal Journey

The pathway to becoming a designer can be as ephemeral as attempting to define design itself. For many, the allure of pursuing a career in the creative industry is the lack of a formal pathway; unlike medicine or law where one must study for a dedicated period of time, culminating in a ceremony defining moment and resulting in officially being named a doctor or a lawyer. The designer can choose their own pathway, which may not include formal education at all. The beauty of the design industry is the lack of structure it possesses. However, the difficulty of the design industry is the lack of structure it possesses; both the greatest strength and the biggest weakness.

Whilst in theory anyone can become a designer, the reality is that it still remains an undiversified arena, where the power of networks and relationships provide routes in. The lack of a formal pathway creates the potential for an identity crisis; unlike medicine or law, there is no authoritative moment when an apprentice or student will officially be named a designer. At what point is a designer a designer? When does the seminal moment take place? When does someone become a designer?

Design is lacking a rites of passage experience and thus has the potential to cultivate imposter syndrome. It could also be argued that the discipline of design itself also harbours an identity crisis which in turn plays into the difficulty of defining design. Where law and medicine have their own codes of practice and Hippocratic Oath, design has no such code. Indeed design is afforded remarkable freedom with very little accountability. No doubt design has contributed to great innovation and improvement across history, however it has equally contributed to much darker chapters of human history.

The designer who desires to contribute creativity to social change must be mindful of the industry they are part of, and ensure that in the absence of a universal design code, they must work hard to establish their own. A healthy exercise for any designer should be to establish their own code, perhaps starting as was suggested earlier with 'do no harm.'

To this end, the designer must define their own practice. In doing so, the designer can not only shape their own design code, but begin to negate the imposter syndrome by building an accountability to the society the designer is seeking to serve.

A practice represents the portable studio of a designer, that which the designer carriers within them at all times; processes and methodology, values, ethical considerations, beliefs and understanding. Without the articulate establishment of accountability in the life of the designer we risk doing harm in the pursuit of doing good. Defining a personal code can help in fluency for the language of endings as accountability lines can be drawn and articulated.

Speaking Truth

The imperative nature in including honesty and humility within the values of a designer, is to ensure we can be truthful and humble enough to determine the ending of our own role within an initiative, and to ensure we are able to perform that ending carefully and sensitively. How we design ourselves out of that which we design is as important, if not more, than being involved in creating impact in the first place. Indeed the purpose of ensuring we, (as designers), fashion a set of values that both reflect our behaviour whilst also pointing towards aspiration, is to ensure we are factoring-in robust mechanisms to behave in a way that is always looking to reduce the harm we may cause.

At the tragic conclusion of Arthur Miller's, *Death of a Salesman*, the audience is left saddened and shocked, which should tell us that even when we are being signposted towards a sad ending, we are still woefully under prepared to deal with it. As designers we must become literate in endings, and the semiotics of endings, in order to provide the language to discuss the phenomena.

Contemplating Endings
The growing proficiency regarding the competencies demonstrated in our literacy of endings must be strengthened at the beginning of all our conversations and absolutely not a bolt on or afterthought. To begin something by discussing how it may end, sounds counterintuitive, however, by initiating the space for closure, we are able to build with a freedom that supports the conditions of a safe and enabling environment.

It is problematic to create the space for dialogue concerning endings, without contemplating our own ending. All things end, as will our lives, however what has been of huge significance for my own practice has been the adoption of 'cathedral thinking'. A concept that originated from the medieval era when great cathedrals were constructed. The theory revolves around the idea of long-term planning, patience, and collaboration to achieve a grand vision. It is a mindset that focuses on creating something extraordinary, which often takes generations to complete.

It is equally important to remember that the ending of something is rarely the end of everything; the end of a marriage isn't the end of love and the end of a journey, isn't the end of adventure. Biomimicry teaches us that the ending of life can sustain further life and that nature might view a relationship with endings more organically. As we can begin to make better relationships with endings, we will be able to contribute to better social change across the world. A founder knowing when to step aside, a designer knowing how to design themselves out of the initiative are examples of the scope we should be encouraging.

Making Sacrifices

Ensuring all are part of the conversation requires the designer to be able to gather people, host people and provide the space for effective dialogue. How we curate and create the safe and enabling environments to define such a space requires a deeper understanding of the social areas we have chosen to contribute towards.

We discussed earlier the importance of both visible and invisible sacrifices, these are inherent attributes that will not only model an understanding of endings but provide the designer with a greater language of endings. The more the designer sacrifices, the more exposed they are to endings. Fluency in how we sacrifice increases our vocabulary of endings.

Understanding the language of neighbourhoods and the rituals of the people in those neighbourhoods takes time, which in of itself is a sacrifice. Care must not be compressed and the work of the socially driven designer has the fingerprints of care all over it. The eloquence in understanding new cultural languages provides the designer with the skills to; invite, gather and host a safe and enabling space for conversations to take place for all. The more the designer applies care, the more their vocabulary of endings increases.

Motivation and Compassion

Mirrors reflect our behaviour, however behind our behaviour lies our motivation. The designer must dig beyond behaviour to explore their own motivations. As Ruskin identified in the *Seven Lamps of Architecture*[40], the internal journey of the designer defines what the designer will make. The internal journey schools the designer in the language of endings.

"Know thyself", a maxim attributed to Socrates, inscribed upon the Temple of Apollo in the ancient Greek precinct of Delphi is equally as relevant to the socially driven designer of the twenty first century.

---

[40] John Ruskin, The Seven Lamps of Architecture, 1989 Dover Publications, UK

We fear that which we do not know and the internal journey of the designer is to know thy self in order to contribute toward the ending of negative phenomenon and creation of positive collaboration.

In choosing to become an empathetic designer or a compassionate craftsman, we become familiar with the discourse of endings, providing us with the scope for healthier beginnings.

I am reminded of Schumacher's quote: "how mans needs are infinite but materialism is finite. Infinite comes only from spirituality.[41]" There is a gap, a delta, a shortfall between what man possesses and what he needs. Aristotle believed that moral excellence comes about as a result of habit. We become 'just' by doing 'just acts', temperate by doing temperate acts, brave by doing brave acts. The process of doing something, and doing it frequently, develops our ability to improve, to do it better, to do it well. The gap, therefore, can be bridged by our own action of doing, by practicing that which we have crafted, honed and are motivated to do. We all have a practice; we all have beliefs, skills and ways of doing things, and Sennett argues for the craftsman in all of us to be freed, to make articulate our practice and in doing so become naturally fluent in the language of endings.

We have arrived at the end of the internal journey, and my hope is that three clear themes have been communicated to the reader.

Define Design
The value of defining what design means to you. The process of defining design unlocks a new vein of personal agency, where the designer is able to articulate the kind of design they might have dreamed of. Defining design has an additional value that I have personally experienced, when a member of the

[41] E.F Schumacher, Small is Beautiful, 1973, Vintage, UK

community you are collaborating with asks you 'why are you here and what does design even mean?' Being able to answer these fundamental questions with authenticity and transparency will require the designer define design for their own practice.

Relationship with Design

We explored how the socially driven designer must build a relationship with their definition of design. In my practice, design is a conversation, therefore my relationship with design is led by the attributes and values that can aid meaningful conversations. Across this chapter we explored a range of values that can advance a foundational relationship between the designer and the practice of design.

I am aware that the themes we explored in this section concern themselves with the nature of the human being, and to a greater degree our values are shaped by our own life experiences, our priming and childhood. However, we can choose to be better versions of who we are and in doing so, we can become better designers in the process.

The designer, therefore, by growing their own understanding of self, becomes more adept at shaping these conversations with a view to draw in others. Through mastering the language of loss - focusing not just on what is wrong with the ending but what is strong too - we established the role of the designer as craftsman, and the work of the socially driven designer as craft.

The Language of Endings

Finally, we explored how defining design and building a relationship with design, organically nurtures a fluency in the language of endings.

A contributing factor to becoming a better version of myself is the active involvement other people, just like in Manet's *Music at the Tuileries* or Ruskin's *Law of Help*, other people are a contributing factor to my development. Through seeing everyone as part of my own development, the possibility for understanding self in relation to others can equip the designer to see the beginnings and endings that the scope of our lives can touch.

I can only be the best version of myself when everyone else has the access to be the best version of themselves. However, we discussed the work of the socially driven designer is not to fix people, but to provide the space - through crafted conversations - to collaboratively reclaim agency that may have been hidden, perhaps since birth.

The interior journey educates us in the language of endings, by underlining our own endings. However, cathedral thinking, can draw the designer to craftsmanship. Craft allows us to better understand endings whilst being true to ourselves and co-create the conditions for change to take place, not the change itself.

In establishing conversations, the designer can familiarise themselves with the syntax of endings; reflection, motivation and sacrifice, for these will not only shape the designer's own practice but help them identify similar attributes when crafting conversations about endings. The society driven designer will always spend their time travelling on an internal journey of reflection, definition, change and loss.

T
R
A
N
S
I
T
I
O
N
S

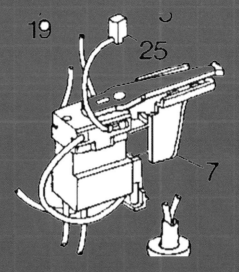

19

25

7

Transitions

After every ending and before each beginning, there is something in-between, the duration and quality of which is utterly variable. The transition between night and day, the loneliness between a love lost and a new love found or convalescing between the gradual ending of a challenging time and the hope for a better season. Transitions are an integral feature of the creation sequence, the final undoing of threads that fall from what had been, before the newly formed seams are re-stitched together in preparation of what could be.

For the socially driven designer these in-between spaces can provide the perfect juncture for meaningful and rich collaboration. Transitions can enable legitimate change. Transitions supply the designer with a social aperture, making sense of endings before making beginnings.

Learning is a transition. Ending the state of being unaware or ignorant and beginning the frame of acquired knowledge requires a transition of learning. The practice of the socially driven designer is dependent on values to guide the interior journey and learning to shape the exterior journey. Mastering transitions through understanding how we learn permits the designer to operate skilfully at pace.

Across this second movement we will be examining transitions in three parts: 1 *understanding phenomena*, 2 *understanding conversations*, and 3 *the Social License*. Across the first part we will be investigating the activity of research as a means of sense making, which will lead us into discussing the hierarchy that understanding possesses over knowledge. Transitions by their very nature are fluid spaces, so too our learning must be flexible in equipping us to stimulate open ended dialogue as we seek collaboration.

For society driven design, collaboration within the space of research is critical, we cannot begin to understand the phenomena unless we are in meaningful dialogue with those who are experiencing the phenomena.

In the second part we investigate the conditions for conversations that can invite significant collaboration. I will share how understanding conversations will educate the designer through deepening their literacy of value exchanges and rituals.

The final part of this movement will be dedicated to legitimising the art of collaboration - in a new way, that is actually a very old way. A journey that will begin by exploring the historical prominence of the Guilds. How they were able to harness profound collaboration, and how we might learn from this. I will be concluding by introducing a new way of validating long form collaboration; the Social License. In-between these themes I will be sharing principles of collaboration and exploring the transitional relationships between business and social change through a history of corporate social responsibility.

Transitions Part One
Understanding the Phenomena

From scientists to anthropologists and from lawyers to venture capitalists, the word research - whilst posing different approaches, is familiar and essential. We undertake research in order to understand something and as a result, how that understanding might better inform our choices. Research could be employed toward a range of scenarios from de-risking an investment to establishing a medical cure.

For the socially driven designer we can explore how research is formed and informed across conversations revealing understanding over three states. *Understanding the phenomena.* We will be exploring how we can make sense of a phenomena through differing elemental states and the ability to make the familiar appear unfamiliar. *Understanding relationships with the phenomena.* Through examining how people, services, systems and systems of systems relate to a phenomena. *Understanding the sequencing of the phenomena.* Finally by exploring where phenomena takes place in the sequence of societal life, we are able to identify points of intervention.

The conversation about research must be broad and diverse in order to capture the extremes of a deficit and an asset approach, thus research should be both problem finding, and strength finding. For many of us the process of research is a naturally familiar one, indeed at some point or another, we have all assembled information, evaluated our findings and made choices based on what we have learnt. The brain constantly makes new pathways by gaining experience, constructing assessments and changing behaviour - touching something hot, and learning from the experience by actioning future avoidance is a tacit and iterative research process.

The quality of the artefact that the socially driven designer makes is often heavily reliant on the quality of research that has been undertaken. The socially driven designer is deeply dependent on collaboration and learning from the experience of others in order to familiarise themselves with the phenomena and in doing so gain a superior quality of understanding. Subsequently the designer must craft conversations across the stakeholders who occupy the phenomena. Conversations that unlock understanding. Designing safe conversations with stakeholders where they are able to recount their known experiences is amazing, however it requires real craft to shape nuanced conversations whereby stakeholders can unlock embodied knowledge; making visible what was once invisible.

Liquid Understanding
In the previous movement we explored the first feature of a designers practice; their values. The designer must determine a definition of design in order to assemble a relationship with design that can include aspirations, behaviour and accountability. The second feature of the socially driven designers practice is 'understanding' - how we are able to learn and how we are able to learn new ways of learning. This is the socially driven designers ability to ask the right questions, expertly interpret a range of answers and draw insightful conclusions. 'Understanding', within the designers practice, is an essential feature of making sense. Making sense for the designer and facilitating the art of sense making for others too.

In everyday conversation one might associate the word, 'understanding' as the ability to perceive the intended meaning of something. 'I think I understand this now' is a phrase that may be taken as a person acknowledging their comprehension of something.

However understanding can play a much more dynamic role in the designers practice - that of fusion. The socially driven designer is able to approach research without having to follow any traditional rules, doing so with innovation and thus creatively plotting unique ways of sense making specific to the phenomena. Unique ways of hosting conversations as research.

Knowledge is what we know, understanding is the marriage of what we know *and* what we do not. For the socially driven designer, understanding should hold a superior place to that of knowledge.

Knowledge is representative of what we know, and that which we know provides us with confidence. Knowledge can be relied upon, dependable, concrete facts, indeed solid in matter, perhaps even with the physical properties that are defined by solids; structural rigidity and resistance to change, all of which is re-assuring as we invariably build upon knowledge.

However knowledge can also represent things that we know, but we are somehow unable to articulate. Perhaps you have experienced knowing something without being able to communicate it using words? My work across prisons and homelessness has taught me that many of those who are working within challenging circumstances or indeed experiencing challenging circumstances, rarely have the opportunity for processing or reflection and thus their accumulated knowledge rapidly becomes embodied. Known but unable to be articulated, and as such they become unaware of all that they know. Knowledge therefore, can be known and unknown, articulated and tacit.

It is difficult to estimate our tacit knowledge as it can often remain inert until needed, however its value is significant in our everyday lives. For the socially driven designer tacit knowledge provides the opportunity to work at a faster pace, but it's harder to build upon as we are incapable of vocalising it. If articulated knowledge has the physical property of a solid, then tacit knowledge resembles the state of a semi solid; retaining a degree of structure but still viscous, somewhat vague or ambiguous. What we know therefore, is a blend of what we can articulate and what we cannot. Solid and semi solid.

What of ignorance, the knowledge that we do not yet possess? Picture knowledge as standing on a hill. Somedays it's perfectly clear, however somedays there's light mist or heavy fog. Sometimes we are aware of the knowledge we are missing, indeed we can almost see it, like a misty morning. Being able to identify what we do not know allows us to pursue the missing knowledge strategically.

Other times however, we are completely ignorant to that which we do not know, and thus unknown knowledge becomes invisible to us, like vapour - oxygen. A complete lack of knowledge is the most evanescent. What we do not know, and are not yet aware of, is utterly undetectable to us. Remaining invisible until we are able to identify it, revealing its fog like properties, making it detectable, knowable.

The four elemental states of knowledge: solid, semi solid, mist and vapour form a symbiotic relationship with each other. The designer must be able to assess their own understanding at all times; being aware of knowledge that can be articulated, knowledge that is embodied and knowledge that is absent. The fusion of all these states creates more than knowledge, it creates understanding.

Understanding is fusion. The marriage of what we know and what we do not. Understanding is maintaining the perpetual state of knowledge and lack of knowledge within liquid form. Research must not just be about solid knowledge, but it must allow the space to make sense of what we know but cannot articulate and that which may escape us altogether.

In this sense Understanding is the fifth elemental state; the constant liquid condition. The society driven designer must ensure that research always maintains its liquid state of 'understanding', never cooling too much that it becomes fully solid, nor should it heat up too much that it becomes ephemeral and gaseous. Our job is to maintain the tension of liquidity. Understanding means the designer does not need to force knowledge from one physical property to another. Too often when research does not provide all the answers for a range of reasons, we may feel obliged to push through knowledge that hasn't been fully realised. Approaching understanding as 'liquid', liberates the designer, permitting them to mix tacit, explicit and unknown with confidence. By maintaining this liquid state we allow understanding to make peace with what we know and what we do not know.

Understanding as a liquid state facilitates our ability to make sense of things with creativity and ambiguity. Before we can make, we must make sense. Understanding is a perpetual transitional state. Mastering understanding, permits the designer to master transitions.

Understanding as liquid form provides us with something that solid knowledge cannot - the scope for meaningful dialogue with all the stakeholders. If design is a conversation across space, time and culture, then research as liquid understanding provides the syntax, vowels and consonants to form meaningful conversations. We are free to be honest about what we do not know and equally liberated to explore conversations that appear obscure or even paradoxical. A liquid understanding enables the designer to approach, the craft of making conversations with greater care and awareness. Before we design anything, we are designing conversations. Conversations that are too fluid to be captured by design tools and even attempting to do so would be a reductive process.

However design tools and traditional research can still be applied through the elemental states. Big data approaches to research - such as carefully prepared surveys and questionnaires with the space for multiple choice or yes /no responses, issued to a large amount of people - can often deliver a solid state of knowledge.

*Sometimes we are so aware of the knowledge we seek,
we can almost see it, like a distant fog or a misty morning.*

Whereas a small data approach; such as long-form interviews and in depth case studies, featuring open ended questions and space for reflection may have a more viscous feel and thus could be viewed as semi solid. The blend of big and small data provide us with a healthy mixture for decision making, but what of fog, knowledge that we know exists but we are unable capture?

Warm data, is a term I first came across in a lecture given by Nora Bateson[42] at The Royal College of Art, who referred to warm data as trans-contextual information. In the context of my practice, the limitations of both big and small data are problematic: we either know a lot about a small group of people, or very little about a big group of people - a generalisation of course - but when access to people is limited and the designer is in need of greater understanding in order to build conversations across space time and culture - we need to access misty knowledge. When attempting to understand a particular community I have applied a warm data approach; learning about a neighbourhood through carefully observing their relationship across the arts. What films are they making or what films are they watching? What kind of music is inspiring them and what kind of musical expressions are they creating? What does fashion look like to this neighbourhood; what are they wearing and how are they wearing it? What is being designed or repurposed? What is being shared? What are they reading or writing? Warm data captures more than the articulated knowledge of a neighbourhood. Warm data is culture, the arts, language, heritage, customs, rituals and rites of passage. The designer does not have to follow traditional research methods and the designer does not have to abandon them either. The designer is free to pick up and put down any knowledge revealing process in the construction of liquid understanding.

A liquid understanding approach to research can be helpful in identifying epistemological error - when negative knowledge passes for actual knowledge. There is a possibility we can incorrectly build on something that isn't concrete, this is known as epistemological error.

---

[42] Nora Bateson, Warm Data, The International Bateson Institute, 2023 https://batesoninstitute.org/warm-data/

However, by applying a liquid understanding, we are able to hold the error alongside instinct, or tacit knowledge and warm data too. All the other states can work to verify or reject information that is held in the tension of liquid understanding. Indeed, liquid understanding can help to mitigate epistemological error.

When I was researching the criminal justice system, a widely agreed concrete example of knowledge was that a guaranteed PAYE job for a prison leaver would reduce recidivism. Taken as solid knowledge, it is natural that we build initiatives on this concrete fact, shaping activities that are designed prior to release from prison. As a result there are some programmes delivered in custody that train prisoners and connect them to jobs upon their release.

However, the chances of someone not going back to prison by walking into a PAYE job is only 9% more likely[43]. There is no doubt that having a job is a contributing factor to reducing recidivism, however, employment is not an 'intervention' that *prevents* re-offending, this is an example of knowledge that simply isn't solid. When re-offending costs the UK government in excess of £18bn per year[44], having a solid fact, that is less than solid, is a dangerous building block to use as a cornerstone.

Liquid understanding provides us with the space to explore and even challenge the quality of knowledge that we are presented with. Observing knowledge across time and culture - what may be solid at one point in time, may be less so at another; therefore by holding our understanding in liquid tension, the designer is able to endorse iterative conversations across space, time and culture.

'Liquid understanding' can provide us with a perpetually fresh language by which to communicate and critique.

---

[43] https://www.gov.uk/government/news/thousands-of-offenders-in-work-as-uk-businesses-help-break-cycle-of-crime

[44] https://www.gov.uk/government/news/thousands-of-offenders-in-work-as-uk-businesses-help-break-cycle-of-crime

For the designer seeking to craft conversations that evoke collaborations, they must ensure the scope of the conversation is accessible enough for everyone to contribute through their own reasoning, rationale and reflection. Whilst a conversation has the breadth to be the most socially equitable approach to design, not all who are invited to speak may have been afforded the agency to do so. Indeed they may have never been modelled the social agility to feel safe and enabled within a conversation across a diverse group of people. The designer therefore, must maintain 'liquid understanding' in order to facilitate fair discourse, by holding in tension knowledge and lack of knowledge the conversation can remain broad, inviting and attractive to a much wider group. Designer as social architect.

The designer must also become a social surveyor - creating the space for conversations, by flattening the ground to elicit a dialogue that is accessible for all.

The approach for the designer as social surveyor should be one of dialogic groundwork. Predicting where the mountains in the conversation require flattening - mountains that may roadblock the natural flow of a conversation. The designer must identify the social landscape, levelling and building as they craft conversations.

Identifying where topics that may be difficult to articulate freely, due to their ephemeral nature may require some rubber scaffolding. The designer as surveyor must be committed to shaping large social infrastructure by unpacking what might be difficult for people to express in words. Once again, the approach to knowledge and research as liquid understanding provides the designer with the flexibility to shape multifaceted conversations.

I recall an example of social surveying when I was embedded in a decade of work across homelessness. We held small group introductory sessions for newcomers in the living rooms of our volunteers many of whom we had previously housed. Flattening mountains, and building up confidence through conversations where trust was built from the get go. This approach was actually suggested to me by one of the first people I housed, partly as a way of them being able to give back as they would bake the most amazing Tarte Tatin, and partly as a way of signposting what we are able to offer through tangible living proof.

Perhaps you can now see the importance of defining a clear relationship to design as stressed in the first movement. The designer, who is operating with kindness and empathy, is naturally able to meter the conversation at the speed of compassion. Thus absolving all from the burden of pressure to arrive at specific answers or datum points that need to be attained. Moving a conversation at the pace of compassion is to offer patience and promote dialogue through ambiguity. The kind of ambiguity that Manet painted in, *The Railway*, allowing for all who viewed the painting to imagine their own future and not feel coerced to arrive at a prescriptive answer.

Re-Order
Humans need order, without it, there would be unmitigated chaos. Order allows us to operate with a sense of stability, enabling us to communicate and learn. Order allows towns and cities to function, grids to generate and systems to deliver.

Sometimes the lack of appeared order, is an order in of itself - that drawer at home where everything seems to live. When our learning is ordered, we are able to retrieve information from when needed - order, helps us make sense of life. Where we place information, is an indication of how we order. How we choose to order our kitchens, or how we might go about arranging a day requires us to place things in specific areas. Pots and Pans in a certain cupboard, or planning a day around meetings or meal times. We are ordering our lives constantly.

As designers, our ability to order is imperative, as we are regularly gathering information that needs to be stored logically. For the society driven designer, how we choose to order information can be a significant factor to the success of our practice.

Humans are unique and thus we will all order information differently - indeed that's the point - as designers, we must order our research creatively, imaginatively and with the openness to detect our own biases. However it's worth noting that socially driven design, guarantees heterogeneous thought due to the diverse nature of the collaborators.

My dear friend and fellow designer, Justin W Cook[45] - who founded the Center for Complexity at Rhode Island School of Design - is a master of re-ordering. He talks passionately about the significant role that designers have to adopt in creatively re-ordering their research. Justin consistently reminds me, that I am free to order my research in any manner I desire. Humans need to order, but modern society has become so acclimatised to stability that we are resistant to change our ordering system.

The reason we get stuck in the way we order is because, there is huge value to creating order - namely survival! Our ability to organise and store information in a specific place, presents us with the time to focus on more unstable aspects, like identifying problems. The designer must not only maintain liquid understanding, but also learn to become fluid in ordering.

In Greta Gerwig's 2023 film, *Barbie*[46], the, 'stereotypical Barbie', at the end of the film, challenges re-ordering by wishing to be the one imagining the idea, not the idea that has been imagined. Gerwig's own re-ordering process of a patriarchal society provided the opportunity for the characters in the movie to create their own change.

Within the liquid state of research, we must create the mechanisms that allow us to navigate away from label thinking, that may restrict our ability to 'understand'. Order has a tendency to gravitate towards knowledge, which can then tend to cool our liquid understanding to the point it becomes solid concrete and our ability to re-order is severely hampered. As designers we already have the scope to re-order

---

[45] Rhode Island School of Design, Center for Complexity, 2022 https://complexity.risd.edu/

[46] Greta Gerwig, Barbie, 2023, Warner Bros

our thinking - Lulu Miller's excellent book - *Why Fish Don't Exist*[47], cleverly takes the reader on a journey of order, chaos and re-ordering. She diligently challenges our established taxonomy of nature, causing us to think and even consider that which we thought we knew. Miller takes that which is concrete, as knowledge, and makes it disappear completely. She points out that we already have a hard-wired process that can naturally challenge ordering. The designer should not blindly accept the reality they are presented with, even if many are happy to accept the labels they are given. The goal for the society driven designer is where possible to maintain liquid understanding across all elemental states, never cooling so much that thinking becomes frozen and never heating up too much that thinking becomes completely ephemeral.

John Ruskin, like Alexander Van Humboldt, the 18th century explorer, chose to re-order how they viewed planet Earth[48]; by suggesting that the world contained only one species - and that is nature - all living beings are merely a part of this one species - nature. Re-ordering, allows us to transform the familiar, into the unfamiliar; thereby revealing the potential for what may have been hidden before. Often when undertaking a new project we are may find ourselves gathering enormous amounts of information and in attempting to develop understanding there is a danger we may drown in an ocean of research, unable to make salient decisions due to information overload. In order to avoid this occurrence we must practice the art of re-ordering constantly, challenging our own norms, by creating fresh taxonomy. In practice this may look like breaking down the enormous amount of information into much smaller sub headings, the names of which can always change. Fresh taxonomy, ordering and re-ordering provides the designer with the headspace to view an ocean of information clearly, quickly and effortlessly.

47 Lulu Miller, Why Fish Don't Exist, 2020, Simon & Schuster

48 Andrea Wulf, The Invention of Nature, 2015, John Murray, UK

This process of re-ordering our understanding so we may challenge our own perspectives is beautifully demonstrated through the poetry of Sylvia Plath.

"What I fear most, I think, is the death of the imagination... If I sit still and don't do anything, the world goes on beating like a slack drum, without meaning. We must be moving, working, making dreams to run toward; the poverty of life without dreams is too horrible to imagine." - Sylvia Plath.[49]

De-familiarisation is the poetic technique that pushes readers into a viewing space where the once familiar becomes strange and unfamiliar. This process can change or enhance the interpretation of the reader. Plath takes her audience on a journey that makes the ordinary appear new, by re-arranging core elements of our social architecture. In this sense Plath is echoing Aristotle, who once wrote: "Poetic language must appear strange and wonderful.[50]"

What would it look like if the National Gallery in London's Trafalgar Square decided to re-order their entire collection, by only featuring artwork that contained white peonies? Or what if the Natural History museum re-ordered their entire collection based on colour; everything that orange is featured at the entrance (replacing the T-Rex), followed by everything green - how do you think people would respond? The point of re-ordering isn't to question the logic behind the changes, but to reveal something we do not yet know. To reveal a new truth.

I have ordered research for a project based purely on things I learnt on Mondays; 34 Mondays to be precise. By arranging and re-arranging information we are increasing the chances of seeing something that could have been missed, or identify something that has never been seen previously; the rarest of sightings - a fresh insight.

_____

[49] Sylvia Plath, Johnny Panic and the Bible of Dreams: Short Stories, Prose, and Diary Excerpts, 1977, Faber

[50] Viktor Shklovsky: A Reader. 2017, Bloomsbury

However it's important that we do not become precious about re-ordering, the beauty of taxonomy is that it helps us understand that there are many ways to view something, and it's helpful never to get stuck in only one way of doing so.

By embracing liquid understanding, re-ordering, should be seen as *a* way of making sense, but never *the* way. The designer must challenge themselves to ensure their newly acquired understanding stands alone, free from bias or misled interpretations.

Factors of Transition - Speed, Scope and Scale
Today we view social innovation as a technical issue, where our problem is often perceived as idea scarcity. If only we had more ideas, we would be able to solve more problems. The Medieval Guilds, demonstrated social innovation as an upstream concept. The challenge becomes less about scarcity of ideas and more about creating the conditions for communities to speak freely and creatively.

Speed
In Alvin Toffler's, *Future Shock*[51] he shared, how the rapid speed of technological change was outpacing human comprehension. He portrayed an image of humanity being left behind - a social paralysis induced by lightning technological change. Toffler highlighted the speed of technological change and human understanding, in doing so he also demonstrated that all industries possess a speed of change.

For the socially driven designer approaching every phenomena with an understanding of its unique clock speed - the rate at which it changes - becomes significant in navigating transitions.

Phenomena, like the re-offending rate for example, are housed within a system that lives within a system of systems.

---

[51] Alvin Toffler, Future Shock, 1970, Random House

Re-offending, the rate at which people who are released from prison return to prison, lives within His Majesty's Prison & Probation Service, (HMPPs), a system that is part of the Ministry of Justice, a larger system, which is part of our Government - a system of systems. Systems also have clock speeds of change - the speed at which the government creates policy and reform for example. Understanding how quickly change takes place across these systems provides the designer with an indication of the speed required for their intervention.

The clock speed of technological advancement, as stated by Toffler, could be seen as rapid, especially if we choose to zoom in and focus on the speed at which operating systems, (OS) for smart phones are updated. The speed of the technological system, facilitates intervention to take place at an equal tempo. A smartphone's OS can be updated and upgraded on a monthly basis. This speed of change enables a range of different possibilities, from better performance, to the compatibility with new and smarter apps. In comparison the clock speed of governmental change, needs to be much slower, risks must be mitigated in pursuit of creating safer communities. Subsequently the rate at which government operating systems are updated could take decades and the compatibility with international laws may take an age to ratify. Of course the impact of policy is far more profound than bug fixes for a new OS, however, for the socially driven designer, understanding the speed of the phenomena in relation to the proposed clock speed of change, becomes an important aspect to understanding the phenomena.

If the speed of change cannot outpace the speed of the phenomena, additional measures must be taken. The clock speed of homelessness runs faster than the clock speed of change within homelessness; the initiatives created in order to ameliorate homelessness cannot operate quick enough. This does not necessarily mean the initiatives are not working, it simply signifies that the interventions are unable to keep up with the velocity of the phenomena.

The recidivism rate in the UK is around 60%,[52] which means approximately six out of every ten people released from prison across the United Kingdom, will return to prison within a year. If we wish to see positive change within the criminal justice system we need interventions of change to operate quicker than the clock speed of the phenomena. The clock speed of design, therefore, needs to be even quicker than a 60% re-offending rate. The quicker these interventions are launched, the quicker society will benefit from the impact, the less victims of crime and the increase of safer communities. Speed, in this instance, is equal to justice.

To understand speed, the designer must manage time and in doing so, time must be understood if the designer is to collaborate in conversations across space, *time* and culture.

When the phenomena is clearly outpacing the current clock speed of change, we simply do not have the luxury of time. We do not have the time to undertake a three year research project focusing on inner city poverty only to find out that the data we spent thirty six months capturing is no longer fit for purpose.

Society driven design must work hard to ensure research projects, through meaningful conversations with communities, operate in parallel to making tangible initiatives. Stacking our activities in this manner provides the opportunity to short circuit time.

Through collaborative conversations research becomes making and making becomes research.

[52] UK Government Ministry of Justice Proven reoffending statistics: January to March 2021, Published 26th January 2023

In Ancient Greece there were two separate words used to describe time; Chronos and Kairos. Chronos, from which the word chronograph is derived from, measures units of time, seconds, minutes, hours, days, months and years. These are the units that we measure our own lives by, and the units that we tend to measure work and productivity against. The passing of time can be a source of anxiety, as we age, we are more likely to imagine endings and of course contemplate our own ending.

By establishing healthier endings for initiatives through designing effective endings for complex problems, the designer creates the space for endings to have a more accessible route to dialogue. In Greek mythology, is is believed that Chronos consumed his own children in an attempt to stop time; Chronos felt trapped by the limitations of time and believed that in committing this dreadful act he could halt time and thus, halt the ageing process. Chronos time provides us with very limited possibilities and even fewer choices. Chronos is a proxy for the restrictive dimensions that we are often presented with when surveying a project. The deadlines, the end of the week, the close of play.

Kairos operates outside of Chronos. Kairos can view a relationship between two people as an entity outside of time. Kairos doesn't measure the Chronos units of time, it measures the quality of the relationship. An example of this would be to define Kairos as the 'right moment', or 'opportune moment'. It would be odd to measure a friendship in terms of billable hours, to that end, a friendship is measured outside of time, with quality, love, trust and care. Kairos describes rather more conceptual values, where neither possibilities nor choices have been narrowed down by a metric of time, remaining limitless. The limitless possibilities and intangible beauty of a friendship.

Kairos, in the sense of society driven design, becomes the investment into human relationship, through the craft of making conversations, understanding exchanges and the building of new rituals.

The designer will always have to operate in both Chronos and Kairos, being careful to balance the two by employing order and re-order, liquid understanding and the values contained in their practice.

Human connection requires connecting, meaningfully, with crafted conversations - Kairos time, an approach I employ. However I also choose to spend a Chronos unit of time within a phenomena, often ten years. A decade allows me to learn the languages, the nuances, the existing rituals and cultures of a phenomena. This approach is referred to by legendary designer and author, Dan Hill as, *embedding*.

Embedding, as Hill writes, in *Dark Matter & Trojan Horses*[53], aids the anthesis to the concept of 'design thinking'. Embeding is the act of being in a system but not *of* the system. Spending a decade in homelessness allowed me to launch a range of different initiatives, many of which didn't require too much sense making or prototyping, because I had embedded, into the system: the research had become tacit knowledge - semi solid. I was able to operate at a much faster clock speed, acquiring knowledge of the system, allowing me to approach relationships though Kairos time.

Over the last few years within the criminal justice system, I have been able to witness society driven design across a portfolio of interventions, some even outpacing recidivism. Embedding can provide a Kairos trajectory for relationships that still live within the Chronos speed of the service. To make anything of value, the designer must sacrifice something valuable. Oppression can only be eliminated with the participation of the oppressed; and poverty can only be eradicated with the collaboration of the poor, therefore the designer must be designing meaningful conversations in time and outside time. Chronos and Kairos.

---

[53] Dan Hill, Dark Matter and Trojan horses, 2012, Strelka Press

"What I fear most, I think, is the death of the imagination."

Sylvia Plath.

What I fear most, I think, is the death f the imagination... If I sit still and on't do anything, the world goes on eating like a slack drum, without neaning. We must be moving, orking, making dreams to run oward; the poverty of life without reams is too horrible to imagine."

lvia Plath.

e-familiarisation is the poetic chnique that pushes readers into a ewing space where the once familiar ecomes strange and unfamiliar. This rocess can change or enhance the terpretation of the reader.

Scale

When E.F. Schumacher wrote *Small is Beautiful* [54] 50 years ago, the thought of scaling down our growth was a radical notion. Chasing the clock speed of the phenomena, traditional iterations of social change are under pressure to grow initiatives quickly - impact at scale. Scale however, can be problematic.

The growth model of the 20th century required product designers to think big and subsequently, companies would act bigger, achieving healthy economies of scale. This growth created two crucial conditions for scale; dependency on uniform structures and consistent material performance. The adherence of these conditions, made large-scale production possible for the global industrial economy.

Social impact cannot be grown in such a manner, as neither of the two conditions for scale are possible. The dependency that traditional design once placed on uniform structures and materials to grow markets cannot operate to grow social impact, as the uniform structures are rarely uniform, or perhaps uniform only in appearance and the materials are stretched beyond capacity.

Social phenomena cuts an arc across our national systems and services, that do not have the rigidity of global manufacturing or distribution. The benefits system, health system and the criminal justice system, for example, rely on the material of humans to deliver these services. Humans who are stretched to operate beyond their capacity of time. Those on the other end of these services: benefit recipients, patients, and prisoners will invariably find themselves in changing circumstances and environments. Time poor and chaotic circumstance force people into pulling and pushing systems to act irregularly, and in completely non-uniform ways.

We cannot and must not assume social impact can be solved by scaling up, to do so, would be to further stretch these overloaded and unstable systems to breaking point.

---

[54] E.F Schumacher, Small is Beautiful, 1973, Vintage, UK

De-risked scale is possible through developing dependency on non-variable components and systems, which is what InHouse Records became, an alternative micro system that sought to deliver choice and uniform outcomes at a small scale. However when working with real people, who are unique in their responses and behaviour, scale is never straight forward.

As the global economy begins to come to terms with untethering from fossil fuels, how we eat, how we heat our buildings and how we travel, will not only come under greater scrutiny, but the opportunities for change will appear across economic modelling systems. We have a window to explore better ways of tethering sustainability with micro initiatives across our planet. It is not a fresh revelation that small, localised and connected, provides a better way of exploring sustainable living. However it seems to me, that small, has more profound value than ever before.

Small does not mean a small appetite for change, on the contrary small scale can actually uphold the vision for far reaching change and significant impact. A significant societal challenge will rarely be solved by a single iteration, many smaller initiatives however can contribute to solving a complex challenge.

The many complex problems that orbit our society, cannot be solved by scale. Society driven design can provide real change through growth, by providing a portfolio of micro interventions. The desperation of the, 'find-an-idea-that-works-and-scale-it-up' approach is understandable given the speed at which the challenges are outpacing interventions.

In my experience one solution for any societal issue is rarely the answer. Societies are complex, non linear eco-systems that are able to adapt even when some factions of society experience hardship.

Adaptivity is an element of complexity. Complex systems are able to grow and learn as a whole, due to the diverse components operating within. Society driven design must also feature complexity, by ensuring that society is accurately represented across the conversations. In doing so, the conversations will inherently be more adaptive and interdependent.

In addition to adaptivity and diversity, complex systems, like society, bear the hallmark of interdependence, therefore the designer needs to ensure many conversations across the stakeholder group can take place. Many conversations, formed from a liquid understanding and re-ordering of the phenomena, embedded with a Kairos approach to relationships.

The scale of our interventions need to be diverse, adaptive and interdependent. A portfolio of small approaches bears the added advantage of being deployed at a quicker clock speed, and more pertinent to the challenges of traditional scale. A portfolio of small approaches can also be tested and validated at a much faster rate. This is not to say that initiatives that are successful cannot be replicated, however growing initiatives, not scaling them, allows for the initiative to adapt to a wider set of challenges. Kees Dorst in his book, *Framing Concepts*[55], highlights the challenges of attempting to solve new issues with old approaches. Framing our solutions, by delivering a range of prototypes, not only ensures we have an adaptive approach, it also equitably reflects the diverse group of collaborators involved.

A conversation across space, time and culture with diverse collaborators developing a portfolio of possibilities provides the latitude for divergent transitions.

Scope
The borders of any societal issue can be defined by its speed, scale and scope. Scale may often refer to the dimensions of the outcome, whereas scope will often refer to borders of the challenge.

---

[55] Kees Dorst, Framing Concepts, 2015, MIT Press

The complexity of society, with its many moving parts can be likened to the landscape of an ocean[56]. The challenges the society driven designer is attempting to navigate are not fixed like a mountain range, they are constantly dancing, like waves upon an ocean. How can we begin to apply design towards a moving landscape? Perhaps we are able to see the folly of traditional approaches to social change; ignoring the clock speed of the phenomena, designing at scale and creating fixed solutions that are founded in concrete knowledge.

Moving landscapes require flexible micro interventions. Only when we are able to generate meaningful conversations with everyone across the stakeholder group can we imagine initiatives that are as adaptable and diverse as the society they were born from. Scope therefore can focus on the complexity of the landscape.

Boundaries are a normal occurrence in nature - the ocean and the shore, the edge of a forrest and a clearing, the drop of a cliff - these natural boundaries can also provide a lens for the designer to imagine scope as they possess natural transitions from endings to beginnings.

The designer should be encouraged to focus on boundaries within society. A beautiful example of this is the work of Studio L[57]. A community design practice, offering the space for collaboration with local neighbourhoods in the metropolitan areas of Tokyo and Osaka in Japan. Studio L nurture conversations with groups who have often been ignored and thus, the act of listening becomes an act of kindness and compassion becomes a vehicle to understand and transition. As a result, the studio successfully creates the space for conversations to take place and therefore Studio L is able to collaborate across a range of much needed solutions. Their unique approach is not limited to their application of practice but also their innovative engagement across scope, and their ability to see the boundaries in society.

---

[56] Professor Scott. E. Page, Understanding Complexity, 2009, The Teaching Company

[57] http://www.studio-l.org/en/

The studio became aware of local governments dependency on management groups to deliver a range of public services through commissioned maintenance contracts. These contracts were being won by large management groups, who possessed the infrastructure and human resources that allowed them to outsource the delivery of the work, often as zero hour contracts to a de-skilled target audience whilst still making a considerable profit.

One such example was local government parks and maintenance contract outside of Osaka in Nose. Studio L perceived an absolutely natural intersection of design and impact. Why shouldn't a socially driven design studio bid for public maintenance contracts? A studio such as this could almost certainly craft the roles for its employees with more care, indeed a service design approach could certainly make the work and associated tasks more aspirational. By seeing the scope as a boundary, Studio L, were able to bid for and win the parks and maintenance contract. A design agency in Japan, is overseeing the maintenance of a council park! Maintaining the grounds of a park, is an example of viewing the scope as a natural boundary. Studio L's work reminds us that innovation is just as much about deciding *where* design intervenes than merely accepting the place that design is traditionally afforded to intervene.

The Double Diamond
So far we have explored an approach to researching phenomena through developing a liquid understanding of knowledge, the exercise of re-ordering - making the familiar, unfamiliar and surveying the factors of transition via speed, scope and scale. The fourth approach to understanding the phenomena is a design process.

The double diamond, is a methodological process, that can equip the designer to move freely throughout the entire conversation. The double diamond allows the designer to seamlessly interchange across the myriad of roles that is required of them - poet, envoy, ambassador, conversational surveyor, social architect and economist to name a few. Mastery of the double diamond makes the roles so fluid they all become one; the socially driven designer.

Whilst Rinus Michels is generally credited with introducing the double diamond process in the 1970's, the profound evolution of the double diamond, was successfully iterated by Johan Cruyff[58] in the 1980's. The double diamond refers to a footballing team formation, made up of players specific positions on a pitch, echoing the shape of two diamonds.

Football, could be viewed as an example of mutually beneficial exchanges, one that includes collaboration and competition. Football coaches, devise strategies to mobilise their players on the pitch in order to win matches. To that end, like many other team sports, football incorporates the idea of individual players on a team having specific tasks to carry out from their different starting positions on the pitch.

For the society driven designer, understanding at what point design is able to intervene across a phenomena, requires the designer to reflect

58 https://www.coachesvoice.com/johan-cruyff-barcelona-coach-tactics-pep-guardiola/

on the scope, scale and speed. Knowing our starting position when attempting to make sense of a phenomena helps us in establishing the level of impact we may hope to achieve. The point of Total Football is to move so effortlessly between the positions that they cease to become set positions at all as everyone becomes adept everywhere - the society driven designer becomes relatable to everyone - but through the articulation of their values, they always remains themselves.

Studio L explored a very unorthodox starting position - design as local council maintenance contractor. A starting position for homelessness may be anything from collaborating with a local soup kitchen to re-designing policies within a national governmental team.

The starting position for any design conversation will often be dictated, by the factors of transition: speed, scope and scale, as well as the liquid understanding and re-ordering of the phenomena. The designer may feel that working with a local soup kitchen may provide a quicker speed of change than re-designing policy at a governmental level. Each starting position requires a nuanced understanding of exchanges, rituals and conversation that can facilitate collaboration.

The designer may identify a more obscure starting point, one that can provide a different scope within the field of homelessness - perhaps focusing on banking the unbanked, and working with a financial institution to better navigate the factors of poverty? In doing so the designer is changing their starting position and by default requiring different conversational approaches.

The double diamond, re-imagined by Cruyff, equips everyone to know everyone else's role. Whilst this may seem like a straight forward, in the world of specificity this is not. The term often used for those who are skilled in a range of areas is a *generalist*, with the term *specialists* being attributed to those who are considered to have extensive expertise in a chosen field. Cruyff's approach equips every player with the expertise of operating in any position, thus making the positional player a more complete footballer.

Cruyff assumed universal principles for every position that complemented the unique skills that every player possessed. These principles are the ability to pass the ball properly and the ability to control the ball properly. Cruyff would repeat: "you must be able to control the ball, if you cannot control it, you cannot pass it either[59]."

For the socially driven designer, the universal principles relate to being able to host conversations; listening and sharing. The designer must craft value exchanges and fresh rituals in order to make conversations. If the designer cannot easily make conversations anywhere across society, then they will be restricting certain pockets of society from actioning change.

Transitions Part Two
Understanding Conversations

In the first part of transitions we investigated how the designer can make sense of the phenomena. How they can make sense of the phenomena in relation to systems and to people, and finally how they can make sense of the phenomena by identifying where it occurs in a societal sequence (factors of transition). The second part of transitions concerns itself with understanding conversations. Design is a conversation across space, time and culture, our ability to craft these conversations with liquid understanding and re-ordering become critical to ensuring all are able to contribute. To that end we will be exploring themes of value exchanges, rituals and speech as we seek to become masters of conversation for socially driven design.

[59] https://www.coachesvoice.com/johan-cruyff-barcelona-coach-tactics-pep-guardiola/#:~:text="Football basically consists of two,you cannot pass it either."

The Refractive Process

Refraction is an event that occurs when light waves pass through mediums of varying density, such as water or glass. The more dense the medium the more it slows down the speed of the light waves. When light passes through glass, it slows down enough for the human eye to view the different colours contained in a light wave, colours that would have been impossible for our eyes to discern without the use of a medium by which to slow down light.

As designers, seeking to acquire greater 'liquid understanding' of a phenomena, we may well find ourselves operating at a much slower tempo of sense making, compared to those who are living through the phenomena. To make sense of a conversation, we may choose to apply a refractive process; exploring mediums to help us slow down the conversation in order to reveal a myriad of colours previously hidden. The designer must learn to reveal that which was previously invisible.

You may have gathered that tempo becomes an interesting factor to master. How the designer is able to speed up and slow down time will determine a range of outcomes associated with the quality of the conversations. The clock speed of the phenomena, the Kairos of meaningful relationships, the Chronos of embedding. The slowing down of conversations, a refractive practice to reveal the social colours of a people group caught up in a phenomena. Tempo refers to the ability to manipulate time, and one of the most significant skills a designer can nurture is that of mastering tempo. Christopher Nolan uses the concept of time across so many of his films. He demonstrates a mastery of slowing down time, chopping it up, arranging it in non linear formats, presenting time in reverse cycles and even introducing time within sleep as embedded within dreams. These cinematic examples provides the socially driven designer with a healthy range of refractive lenses by which to view a project. From the future looking back, from the past looking forward, or a moment in time viewed across a week, a single day and a solitary hour. Nolan uses the medium of film to slow down our understanding of time, cinema can be a refractive process to understand space travel, the historical narrative of Dunkirk, dreaming and short term memory loss.

The designer can find their own ways of slowing down conversations, by re-ordering different themes in real time. The designer can practice refraction by slowing down a sequence of events that may have been discussed in conversations, allowing their minds eye to view how the situation may have played out differently. Refraction can help the designer understand the range of emotions, circumstances and feelings that reveal a phenomena. A helpful guide to the refractive process and indeed understanding conversations is learning how value exchanges take place across every human interaction.

Exchanges

In his book, *Together*[60], Richard Sennett wrote about the lost art of working together. He likens the skills required for collaboration to that of a diplomat; someone capable of negotiating, remaining calm in difficult situations, working towards an exchange in which the participants can mutually benefit from the encounter.

It is clear therefore, that the work of the designer cannot be passive, as such, tolerance will not suffice, as it often merely provides a mask; tolerance needs replacing with different skills, the skills of a refractive process and the skills that facilitate the designer as diplomat, being able to host conversations across space, time and culture. In this sense the medium to slow down our understanding are the skills for negations, as they reveal the colours of the differing wants and needs.

We are social creatures, statistically we live longer the more meaningful connections we have especially in later life. Our lives are richer for the meaningful connections we enjoy, and these do not always have to be deep connections, as there is great value in the power of weak connections - with those who we may never class as friends. These lighter interactions help us develop different skills, than those used to build more meaningful relationships. Natural everyday collaborations are essential for our own personal development and wellbeing.

---

[60] Richard Sennett, Together, 2012, Penguin, UK

Connection is essential - but maintaining connection is an art, primarily because every connection is vulnerable to instability, therefore we need the skills to maintain relationships in chaos as well as stability. Organisational structures can provide conditions to limit chaos but they cannot guarantee stability. Indeed even the smallest and most ancient organising structure; the family unit, cannot guarantee a life without chaos.

We need each other, yet we do not have a stable structure that supports each other. Exchanges create the space for humans to develop a degree of stability amidst the instability. All primates trade in exchanges, the more intelligent the primate the more conscious we become of what others think and thus we are able to fashion more complex and nuanced exchanges. Exchanges in-of themselves, are well documented and as such, a broad spectrum has been understood and commonly named; ranging from 'self sacrificial' to 'winner takes all' and everything in between. A feature of all exchanges relies on the fuel mixture between collaboration and competition.

To the nine year old version of me, design was truth.
To the seven year old version of me, football was belonging.

As an immigrant from the Middle East growing up in the 1970's, London had its challenges, however one place where my identity was never questioned was on the football pitch. The questions that society seemed to be fascinated with didn't apply when I was playing football. Nobody wanted to know where I was really from. The most obvious question any immigrant is asked; 'where are you from?' And when you respond with a local town you consider to be home, the immediate secondary response becomes, 'no, I meant where are you *really* from?' With football however, I was immediately accepted.

Whilst it may be too simplistic to suggest football as an affinity framework for the designer to study, association football does provide a glimpse of both collaboration and competition in various differing exchanges and thus can be used as an illustration. Football requires the collaboration from all the stakeholders to agree the mechanism and operation of the competition, agreeing the rules of a league or the rules of a knock-out tournament for example. Collaboration is also required by every team scheduled to play each other, they all need to agree on the rules of the game, the duration, the venue, time and date. Competition takes place during a football match between the two teams, but at the same time there also exists collaboration within each team, as players work together to compete against their opponents who are also collaborating. The exchanges in football are never 'winner takes all', as defeat does not represent the end of football. Even teams that lose, don't lose everything, but just enough to remain competitive. Association Football in England, has a 150 year history, many of the teams playing today were formed over a century ago. The value exchanges created within the organisational structures have fashioned a space where the end of a match isn't the end of a club, regardless of the outcome.

As designers, we need to slow down the light of information to reveal the wider colours of a phenomena. Refraction by using the medium of exchanges facilitate this and therefore becoming skilled at exchanges is an important feature of the designers ability to build meaningful and revelatory conversations.

Self sacrifice or altruism, is one extreme of the value exchange spectrum; and is driven by an intense self will, which if truly deep seated, will not seek recognition. One could argue that if anyone seeks recognition for their altruistic behaviour, then their act is no longer altruistic. The exchange for altruism is inherently personal, and should not require broadcasting to a wider audience in order to validate it. On the other extreme of the spectrum 'winner takes all' exchanges are final, and much as they sound, those who lose, lose everything. As the designer making conversations, both extremes are dangerous and should be carefully navigated to avoid arriving at either of these value exchanges.

A balance between 'altruistic' and 'winner takes all' is the 'win-win exchange': an exchange where both parties gain something they deem valuable. Win-win exchanges are mutually affirming, but need to be hedged with necessary caveats, in order to ensure the win is genuinely mutual. The design of these caveats is important as the use of ambiguity can be both a good and bad thing. An exchange seeking to be win-win and deploying ambiguity, with persuasiveness, could result in someone being made to 'feel' good simply in order to be sold something, therefore this could be an illusionary win-win. However, where ambiguity can play a positive role in a win-win exchange, is the circumstance where both parties are genuinely seeking to promote the welfare of the other, even when the exchange may not be fully known.

For the designer seeking to contribute to social change, ambiguity can be a helpful North Star, as it promotes a transparent direction where the actual outcome of the exchange is yet unknown and can only be determined by those making the exchange. In the refractive process, the equitable use of ambiguity in developing change becomes imperative as it provides the air cover to act freely in purist of mutual value.

Rituals
Win-win exchanges require the designer, to master a range of dialogic skills, that can validate and support their practice in unearthing and generating potential value from ambiguity. These nuanced skills are often too intangible to be viewed in isolation, however we find them interconnected across rituals. Therefore, for the designer to master win-win exchanges, they must dedicate themselves to the craft of identifying and creating rituals.

A ritual is often viewed as a sequence of activities involving gestures, words, actions, or artefacts, commonly placed within a ceremony. However, everyday rituals are far more nuanced and live ubiquitously deep within the fabric of society. The designer exploring socially driven design must be able to detect rituals across societies and cultures in order to meaningfully design conversions with all, across space, time and culture.

The first day I walked into a prison I was exposed to a million sounds and sights, too numerous to mention, however upon gradual familiarity, and a growing taxonomy of the criminal justice system I began to view all the activity as a nuanced portfolio of rituals and ceremony; all possessing value exchanges between prisoners and prisoners, staff and staff, and prisoners and staff.

As a teenager growing up in differing places across the Middle East and London, I was able to observe the beauty of everyday rituals. Two men walking toward each other on a busy London pavement; one man raises his eyebrows at the same time as lifting his head in the slightest of nods; he is letting the other know that he poses no threat to him. The other responds by mimicking the greeting but doing so slightly quicker to ensure their is enough time for acknowledgement.

The range of greetings that exist within different communities and across a wide age group can denote the level of friendship or trust that exists. A handshake, one of the oldest everyday ceremonies, is a portable ritual that may be used to seal a promise, or an action to signify a state of peace, or a greeting for friends and strangers. The dimensions of the handshake are varied but its usage is immediately understood by either party. The handshake is a ceremony that has a range of different meanings all of which are understood by society. Thus the designer can make sense of value exchanges, that are represented across different handshakes, in order to design conversations across space, time and culture.

Everyday rituals are nuanced and developed over time. The smile of a kind man, repeatedly enhanced over years, to signify care and compassion. Like a dedicated master craftsman the smiling man is gradually refining their beam, conveying the genuine emotions in the smoothest of facial movements, just like the mastery of a carpenter in the workshop tirelessly sanding down the wooden handle of a tool, ensuring it will perfectly fit the shape of their hand. The kind man smiles his smile a million times; nodding downwards whilst closing his eyes, smiling, as he lifts his right arm towards his chest. The whole ritual takes the kind man three seconds to perform and a lifetime to perfect.

Understanding rituals, allows us to build broader dialogic skills by which to design better exchanges and host meaningful conversations for all to engage with across space, time and culture.

Conversations are a series of meaningful exchanges that need to be designed carefully. Designing successful exchanges requires the craft of balancing co-operation and competition. Rituals, become the equilibrium to these paradoxes.

For the designer to be able to clearly identify rituals, it may be helpful to look at three commonalities that run across all rituals. Firstly rituals rely on a unique repetition or reproduction, a formal example of this could be viewed through religious practices. The Eucharist for example creates a unique repetition; the activity of doing something familiar over and over again, but with each repeat it still bears its own unique experience. The handshake as discussed earlier, is an informal example, maintaining its quality to be unique every time it is deployed. Rituals cannot exist if they are not repeated with meaning.

Secondly, rituals require some kind of symbolism, in the case of the Eucharist there is the icon of the cross, the bread and the wine. Symbolism can be an artefact, or an image, or in the case of a handshake, symbolism is simply the act of two hands joining. Finally, rituals require the use of theatre. The handshake is a piece of social theatre, and more formal type of rituals, like the Eucharist incorporates the theatre of eating the bread and drinking the wine. Rituals thus need some dramatic activity to help us remember them and to set the tone by which we engage in them, they need to be repeated with meaning that preserves their unique aspect each time they are exercised, and they are formed around a symbol that allows everyone to clearly recognise them.

The designer must be able to host conversations that invite collaboration, therefore they must be able to create meaningful win-win exchanges, based on a mastery of dialogic skills and an understanding of rituals. These are the mediums by which to slow down the light of information and dark matter that live in and around culture. The designer must master the art of transitions.

The designer needs to master conversations because the art of collaboration is dying. The designer needs to speak of endings because society does not.

The designer needs to be able to do these well, in order to design conversations that can lead to a better way of imagining our society.

It could be argued that modern work is short circuiting social collaboration. Indeed, since the second industrial revolution one can see how 'work' has de-skilled the populace from engaging in meaningful collaboration. The reduction of 'time' across work can be seen as the biggest significant factor in reducing the space for greater communication and thus effects our ability for meaningful collaboration. Richard Sennett writes extensively on this subject, pointing out that a great deal of our working opportunities in the new economy has a short term time frame.

Task based contracts, constructed as short term projects, bringing people on board for a limited time to achieve an objective before disbanding. Under these specific conditions, co-operation needs to be made explicit, with no time for developing something more profound and thus communication takes the form of declarative speech.

One could argue that these working environments cease to provide the long term experiential base for co-operation and therefore, even the mention of co-creation has become a moral gesture and by no means a genuine social bond. Importantly 'the work' can still happen without the appearance of co-creation and therefore as a gesture, making collaboration a weaker practice. The heightened personalised experience can erode what paltry social bonds exist. The more we make things tailored for individual benefit the more we perpetuate inequality in social dialogue, rituals, win-win exchanges, and by default any realistic chance of social mobility.

Society driven design, naturally rebalances social stock. The designer, crafts the spaces for this to occur through rich and meaningful conversations across space, time and culture.

Collaboration in its essence is working with others doing something that is impossible to do on your own. Children, for example, need to co-operate with those caring for them in order to eat.

society is constantly moving to meet its challenges;
like waves dancing upon the ocean

As adults we are required to co-operate with each other across the workplaces in order to perform our work - however if our work can be achieved with minimal discourse then we are not really collaborating at all. The more co-operation that takes place with other people, the greater the opportunity for engagement with those different to us and as a result the more skills, communication, rituals and exchanges are able to be shared. Designing a conversation, entails portable social behaviour, which the designer should be able to practice anywhere and with anyone.

Speech

These everyday rituals are wrapped up in dialogic skills; from shaking hands, to making eye contact. The designer must therefore not only be skilled in identifying and sometimes even supporting the creation of rituals, but also in moving the conversation across space, time and culture - from inequality towards accessible, enhanced equality. In order to speak into this new conversation, the designer must be aware of the three preferred speech destinations; dialogic, subjunctive and empathetic.

Dialogic Speech

Designers should be encouraged to abate a dialectic approach in favour of a dialogic one. A dialectic approach represents synthesis that ultimately arrives to a consummation. Or put in another way, for a dialectic approach to be successful both parties must be able to articulate, both parties must be able to reason and both parties must be able to arrive at a mutual understanding. This approach makes no exception for inequality, but yet it is the default for professional parlance. This approach is inherent in all didactic task based work, which requires the outcome to be clearly established before the conversation begins. However, as designers seeking to contribute to a better way of being human, society driven design requires genuine collaboration not the optional kind, where the outcomes are often pre-determined.

A dialogic approach requires the designer to develop listening skills to know what the 'other' is saying, especially if they may not have the ability to articulate precisely what they are feeling.

A dialogic approach supports the acquisition of embodied knowledge - semi solid. A dialogic approach does not predetermine a datum, it doesn't need an end, the arrival is the process. In exploring society driven design, we must be open to conversations that are ambiguous, because if we choose to superimpose our own direction, we are influencing the datum before we have even started, and thus, in danger of sub consciously veering towards a dialectic narrative by shaping the outcome before the beginning.

Subjunctive Speech
The designer should be encouraged to minimise declarative talk in favour of subjunctive speech. Declarative speech is a requirement where time is limited. Indeed it is often a feature of small teams involving people that are known to each other for a brief period of time only, working on a short term contract. Forthright language that tends to provide, in the spirit of expediency, limited options, or often binary choices. To be presented with the option of 'in' or 'out' for example is not really a choice if 'out' represents more consequential actions. There are valid reasons why a lot of workspaces employ declarative language, as it helps to communicate actions quickly. It should come as no surprise that the political landscape employs declarative speech.

Subjunctive speech provides the scope for safe and enabling conversations. Subjunctive speech is ambiguous and invites a non-binary approach to conversations that provide limitless opportunity. Subjunctive speech supplies the space for collaboration. Open questions, often employed by mentors or therapists provide the space for thoughts to roam free. Subjunctive speech permits ambiguity in removing the foreclosure of declaration.

Empathetic Speech
Designers should be encouraged to adopt empathy over sympathy. Sympathy proceeds by identification. I am sympathetic by identifying with another person's pain, putting myself in their place.
In effect sympathy, within society driven design, is the act of leaving oneself and imagining what it must be like for another. Sympathy is an essential emotion for understanding ourselves and seeking to

understand others. However in the spirit of collaboration, sympathy cannot be enough, it makes genuine collaboration optional, and collaboration cannot be optional, if we want to see society drive it's own change. Sympathy presumes an understanding without asking.

Empathy, for the designer, is the knowledge that something deeply matters, but unless we ask those who are experiencing the pain, we will always be locked in a guessing game. I cannot imagine what anyone who is homeless or has been to prison will experience or feel, even though for the last twenty years I have dedicated my practice to those two phenomena. I choose not to presume, and thus I choose empathy, not sympathy in the conversations that take place, across space, time and culture.

By simply asking, the designer can learn, to make sense, to build exchanges, understand rituals and shape conversations. Curiosity can be an effective doorway leading to greater empathy. The designer must place themselves in situations where they are able to exercise curiosity. They must also ask of themselves where might those situations might be?

Sympathy on the other hand assumes that nothing is foreign, and that we already know the full capacity of emotions to justifiably design for society. Not that we are concerned with designing anything 'for' anyone, but in order for the designer to build 'with' and facilitate collaboration to create the conditions for design to be driven 'by' society, we are in need of curiosity that begets empathy.

In the building of refractive conversations, the designer should be adept at dialogic skills proceeding without a datum point. The designer should explore subjunctive expression in creating the space for ambiguity and the designer must be empathetic, nurturing the curiosity to learn and never presume. Where once declarative and binary in our choices, the designer must exercise subjunctive expression, providing space for other people's ideas and thoughts. Where society demands a dialectic and transactional approach, the designer can choose to be dialogic; being open to possibilities, initiating conversations towards ambiguous spaces.

When confronted by opportunities born out of sympathy, derived from someone's imagination of what they *think* is right for others, the designer can choose empathy, compassion and curiosity, asking those who have experience of the phenomenon, hearing what they may need and being able to initiate change together. Refraction allows us to see that poverty isn't in the person, it is in the circumstances that surrounds them. Seeing ourselves more clearly, with the opportunity to develop in dialogic skills, allows us to view a wider spectrum of society to embed ourselves in, and a better understanding of what we may have to offer. Gradually, as we make sense of the phenomena and of conversations, we begin to see ourselves more clearly too.

Transitions Part Three
The Social License

The Guilds
The origin of the word 'genius' can be traced back to Ancient Rome, and a collective belief that all people had a guiding spirit, called a 'genius'. A spirit that was in attendance through the lives of everyone. Literally derived from the Latin verb, *gignere*, meaning to give birth or bring forth, 'genius' is the root of the modern day word 'generate' - and in the Ancient Roman sense, was considered a communal activity that would be filtered through an individual. The intangible ideas of a society were transmitted to any individual within that community through the spirit of genius. The spirit was understood to be accessible by anyone, and thus everyone had a genius; the ability to capture a collective idea and breathe life into it.

Genius, in Ancient Rome, provided some fascinating observations concerning the phenomena of ideation. Principally, the responsibility for generating ideas was viewed as active citizenship, thus, a social responsibility. Secondly, with regards to ownership, seeing as the ideas were birthed from the community, the ideas also belonged to the community. Within this culture, providing a fully formed idea was seen as the final phase of a community design process - *we have all been thinking it, but now it has been articulated* - and as such, design itself could be viewed as a community activity, much in the same way a conversation would be better served with more than one person. Genius, enabled conversations to take place across the entire community, since a major factor for innovation to happen would be through the spirit of genius, and that required everyone to engage. The creative commons of Ancient Rome, was not just collective ownership of the idea, but active citizenship in the ideas emergence. Naturally therefore, the most effective vehicle for the spread of ideas across a community was the conversation, deeply embedded within relationships. Creativity was seen as active citizenship.

Before we design anything, we must design conversations.

In modern society the term genius is reserved for individuals, indeed I have never heard of anyone attributing genius to a community or neighbourhood. In addition, the credit for an idea is almost always given to an individual - or at least one or two individuals. In fact the ownership for every phase of an idea is a hotly contested topic, which has resulted in many parts of the world promoting a litigious approach to protecting ideas. Individuals, if legally successful, are able to claim a stake in an idea. We have commercialised the process of ideation. Where once we nurtured a community approach to a creative commons we now have a marketplace for trading ideas. A border controlled space where ownership of an idea can be bought or sold at any stage. This modern approach to creativity does not promote open conversation, rather it thrives on secrecy and independence.

Ideas that may lead to monetisation, will often operate under a spirit of confidentiality, non discourse agreements and copyright protection. Social innovation, however, tends to attract less 'money-making' ideas, perhaps that is a problem in of itself? Ideas that can change society require a different approach to legitimising and recognising value. Too often social innovation is viewed through a 'socially' commercial lens which is problematic as growing change is not the same as growing money.

Ideas within social innovation more often than not require some element of capital to be proven, the process of testing a theory by simply doing it. However, access to the capital to drive innovation is not an easy route. The onus is on the individual to convince funders that their idea is worth investing resources in. It is not my intention to critique the monetisation and thus protection of ideas - indeed money itself is an idea, a social construct - however the process by which to develop ideas that can socially benefit our society, is becoming harder.

We do not have an open culture to speak freely of our ideas with others and accessing any meaningful support to launch these ideas is a crushingly difficult task. Our problems are growing bigger and the resources to solve these challenges are becoming harder to access. We are making social impact very difficult to action.

Physician Gabor Mate[61], hypothesises that we are the only species to actively create the conditions that diminish our own survival. One could go as far as to argue that a societal culture that naturally produces poverty and deprivation - even though the abundant resources exist to negate these - must surely be toxic.

A petri dish, used by bacteriologists, is a small transparent disc, often with a flat lid, used to grow culture of micro-organisms. Mate likens our modern society to a global culture that is grown in an imaginary petri dish, and humans are the bacteriologists that historically keep adding different bacteria, like economic frameworks that affect the culture. Mate suggests that our societal petri dish is poisonous, we need fresh ideas to make positive changes to our society, yet far from making the route to the implementation of these ideas easily accessible, we have fashioned a fractured and inconsistent pathway for social innovation.[62] We are not encouraging the community spaces nor the super fast highways to generate ideas that can implement social change.

---

[61] Gabor Mate, The Myth of Normal, 2022, Vermilion, UK

[62] Gabor Mate, The Myth of Normal, 2022, Vermilion, UK

In Ancient Rome, it was understood that the societal *ether* would provide the conduit to freely bring forth ideas. Ideas that could constitute a better social culture. By nurturing the spirit of genius, the Romans created Collegia's, or what later came to be known as Guilds, deriving from 'geld', meaning to pay or contribute. When we make things well, we are not just creating beautiful artefacts, we are contributing to the growth of society. We are adding good bacteria to the societal petri dish, and doing so together. The process of making teaches us something about ourselves. When we make things together, we all learn something about each other. Guilds could be seen as an unconscious intervention, adding positive contributions to the societal petri dish.

The advent of Guilds influenced cultures in ways that would earn the respect of the public, by harnessing creativity through a refined and educational process. We briefly noted in the previous movement how highly the Guilds were thought of across society that parents would entrust the education and social development of their own children to them. This validation was well founded as children would learn the principles of craft - how to make things, make them well, and make them well together - students not only became craftsmen but also embodied the values of a craftsman, (discussed in the previous movement).

Guilds therefore contributed to society, not just through educating future generations, but through the human development of future generations - when we make things, we learn truths about ourselves, allowing for our own improvement.

In the spirit of Ancient Rome, the Guilds promoted the collective, never the individual, and it was seen as a collective responsibility, not just to provide high quality crafts, but within the Guild, to develop a society of people who valued each other. Guilds of the time, were seen as both community centres and centres of excellence, (somewhere across history these two qualities have separated and in our modern society they are viewed as exclusive functions). Being a community centre and centre of excellence, Guilds were able to create crafts that were desirable as well as meaningfully contributing to society in profound ways. It's difficult to imagine such a place existing today and our societal petri dish is much poorer because of this.

For the last twenty years I have been hosting conversations across space, time and culture with a view to creating the conditions for change to occur. In doing so, I have seen glimpses of the old Guilds, appearing in modern initiatives where together, we are able to rekindle the collective in contributing towards a positive culture by providing the space for community genius, creativity and collaboration.

Interdependence
The process of making, facilitates deeper sense making.
When we make things, truths about who we are are revealed to us.

However making things in a changing world, where the only constant in life is change itself can be tough. The statement "Everything is in flux[63]" feels as relevant today, as it was when Heraclitus put scribe to papyrus over two and half thousand years ago, capturing his thoughts on nature.

All things end. All things are transitioning to either beginnings or endings. We spoke of sense making, ordering and re-ordering earlier in this movement. One could argue the order and re-ordering allows us to build some semblance of structure to provide respite from flux. However, like Mate's example of a petri dish, there are phenomena that do not recognise the man made structures that have been constructed.

The Covid-19 pandemic - like nature - didn't appear to recognise the demarcation lines that constitute our national borders, nor did it appear to care for tourist visas, homeland security or luxury cruises. Nature, like Covid, is oblivious to man-made structures of order.

---

[63] Heraclitus, On Nature, 2010, Kessinger Publishing, UK

Dr Malcom - Jeff Goldblum's rockstar scientist in the 1993 Spielberg classic, *Jurassic Park*[64] - reminds us early on in the movie that "if there is one thing, that history has taught us; it's that life will not be contained. Life breaks free, it expands to new territories and crashes through barriers, painfully, maybe even dangerously, but life...finds a way."

Everything is in flux, working to sustain itself, all life, is trying, to find a way. A constant transition, interrupted with peaks of beginnings and troughs of endings.

Ruskin's 1871 *Law of Help*, promotes the co-operation of all living things in order to sustain life. Everything changes, everything is part of nature and nature adapts by making alliances to sustain life.

Almost five thousand kilometres from Hawaii, where Jurassic Park was filmed, in Utah, is the breathtaking site of the Pando, the worlds largest living single organism. A forest of Aspen trees covering one hundred and six acres, where each tree is connected to each other by one underground root.

The Aspen acts as a living illustration to the truth Heraclitus, Ruskin and Van Humboldt, alluded toward: 'we are all connected.' Indeed more than connected, we are interdependent, mutually reliant on each other. In nature, nothing happens without affecting everything.

One may choose to define complex systems across three attributes: diversity that requires interdependence providing the ability to learn and grow though adaptation. Our society is a complex system and the many neighbourhoods that form our communities possess their own complex systems: interdependent, diverse and adaptive. When neighbourhoods make things, the things they make will inherently contain adaptivity, interdependence and diversity, meaning that what we make together, is not only inherently complex, but more likely to grow stronger in adversity. The art will always inherently carry

---

[64] Jurassic Park, 1993, Universal Pictures, Amblin Entertainment

something of the artist. Whatever the socially driven designer contributes towards, will carry something of them - the need for the social designer to check their own values is imperative as we are also contributing to that social petri dish.

A conversation across space, time and culture allows us to travel east from the Pando in Utah, to Washington DC, and travelling sixty years back in time, to a speech delivered by President Kennedy reminds us that: "We all inhabit this small planet and breathe the same air.[65]" Not only do we share an interrelated relationship with nature, we also experience an integral connection to each other.

Everything is in flux.
Everything is in flux to sustain itself.
Everything is connected.

We are part of nature, interdependent and constantly in flux to sustain ourselves.

A problem we all face is that living in flux is difficult.

Chaos isn't easy to navigate and as a result mankind has sought order to make sense of our lives. Order allows humanity to limit chaos, mitigating a degree of uncertainty, through the creation of systems that provide just enough certainty to help us plan our future days, months and years. These systems arc across every facet of our lives; from social and economic to political and technological, these are the networks that hold everything between us and in-between us.

We know that to make anything, we must sacrifice something. Creating any kind of order from chaos comes at a cost.

What are we willing to lose, in order to gain the comfort of security? Perhaps we have traded our interdependence in favour of personal security? We have appeared to retain our diversity as humans

[65] President John F. Kennedy, commencement address at American University, Monday, June 10, 1963.

and our adaptivity is prominent through our enduring resilience, therefore one may reasonably suggest that we seemed to have forgotten our interdependence. Perhaps more than merely forgotten, which presumes a lapse of memory, our behaviour actually 'acts' as if we are independent. We act as if we are independent to the responsibilities we have to our fellow human beings, we act as if we are independent to the responsibilities we have to our planet.

Living in flux is difficult, but life is made harder by not being around others.

How often have you experienced or heard of someone who, 'feels better simply for talking', the act of processing and living is made easier when in conjunction with the people around us, i.e. 'many hands make light work'. The opposite is also true; fewer hands make heavy work, or we feel worse for not talking about it.

When we act independently, society feels wrong. We can all sense it, perhaps unable to articulate it, but the tacit understanding is there. We feel hurt but we are not sure why. We cry but we are unaware of an apparent reason. Inherently we are interdependent beings, operating in flux, but instead of navigating chaos together, we have been acting independently as if the ordered structure we live by is impervious to change. Something is very wrong if we think and act, separately, when actually we are tethered. We share the same root, much like the Pando in Utah, the consequence of our behaviour, ultimately affects us all.

After a decade of working across the homeless sector, a profound truth was revealed to me; whilst many could survive without shelter and even extremely limited access to food, none could survive without human connection. We may try and act separately but the consequences are severe.

I observed behaviour amongst an impoverished community on the outskirts of Chennai, India, for a brief period in 2010. Many people in tight proximity, with limited nutrition and a severe lack of any sanitation or clean running water. However life found a way - more than that - in the midst of extremely challenging conditions, the mood was not at all oppressive, but actually positive. I couldn't fathom how these extreme living circumstances could generate such a positive outcome. It made no sense to me. One day, perplexed, I sought out the village elder and asked how is it that the community is able to cope with so much stress and anxiety?

His response is etched in my memory, as he smiled - the smile of a kind man - and locked his eyes on mine: "those are western diseases." The more we spoke, the more I learnt, the more I challenged my own notion of community. The best vehicle we currently have to make sense of a nations success is Gross Domestic Product (GDP). However GDP doesn't have the feature to capture stress or anxiety, and more importantly, doesn't detect the absence of it either. GDP tells me something about a percentage metric, even though the UK may enjoy a higher GDP than some northern European countries, the waiting time for an operation may still be significantly longer in the UK compared to countries that appear to have a lower GDP but can provide swifter medical care. What good is a success metric if not to improve the wellbeing of human life? There is no wealth but life.

The community in Chennai naturally recognised what had always been inherent; their interdependence. They were connected, and as such they were a sharing community. Whilst across the standards of the global north, the Chennai community are supremely lacking, but in the designing of conversations for everyone - a conversation about beginnings and endings - they are masterful. Their social cohesion is truly off the charts, the mobilisation of the community could be activated in minutes.

Before travelling to India, I briefly became friends with a Premier League footballer who showed interest in social change, we agreed to meet for coffee and share ideas with no agenda except making sense of what social change meant to both of us. On our very first meeting he confided in me. Me? A stranger to his life. Outside of his network. His life had become so independent that even those closest to him, were actually far from him. He was living and thinking 'separately' - we all do.

Interdependence across community, Chennai, India 2009

Thinking we are separate and living independently provides little opportunities for working out our problems together. Somewhere along the way we traded our interdependence for personal security.

If the individual Aspen trees in the Pando in Utah were to somehow deny their connectivity, believing they can operate with complete independence they would be denying the very root that sustains them all. The consequences of acting with absolute independence seriously affects our personal lives; through a non-exhaustive list that includes matters of wellbeing, debt, network erosion, inequality and prejudice.

I am not dismissing the importance of independence. Autonomy is an essential part of our personal growth, autonomy ensures we are able to operate as our own advocates in society and independence becomes a critical element of development, but only within the knowledge and behaviour that we are simultaneously interdependent.

Socially driven design has a responsibility to make things that highlight our interdependence, as society driven design can only operate in collaboration. The Aspen trees that form the Pando in Utah may need to see their connected root every now and then, just to remember they possess a deep link, always at work regardless of how separate things may appear on the surface, above ground.

Our role as designers in 'making', especially 'making' in a changing world, is to remind all who we are collaborating with. that the alliances we seek are already in place, they just require re-booting. At InHouse we focused on, *what's strong, not what's wrong*. Believing that we are inherently connected, helped us in 'acting' connected. We stopped seeing officers, prisoners and uniforms and began seeing people. Just people, all keen to change their circumstances.

The ghost of Jacob Marley in Charles Dickens' *A Christmas Carol*[66], cautioned Scrooge that mankind should be his business. The novel focuses on miserly Ebenezer Scrooge, a twisted and uncharitable man, who is tormented by three phantoms during one long night, Christmas Eve. The ghosts, in their own way, urge Scrooge to change; the Ghost of Christmas past encouraged change by projecting scenes of Scrooge's youth that prompted deep reflection. The Ghost of Christmas present revealed to Scrooge the inequality and poverty of mankind that Scrooge had neglected to see in real life. The Ghost of Christmas future...well...you get the idea. However, during this epic novel across space, time and culture, Scrooge realised that the person he needed to become, was actually who he had always been or perhaps who he had been denied to become.

Interdependent.

Connected to people and responsible for each other.

Dickens' genius was to illustrate that kindness, forbearance and charity didn't need to be acquired by Scrooge, because they were already inherent in Scrooge. They merely needed locating, dusting off and exercising once more. Like the single root of the Pando has always been present underneath the surface, even if it cannot be seen above ground. Dickens' work urges us to lose our 'separate thinking' and in doing so, uncover our buried interdependence. Life...will find a way.

The shadow cast from Covid-19 should also remind us that if, as a society, we can work interdependently to lockdown something as small and invisible as a microbe, then surely we can work interdependently to lockdown something as ugly and glaringly obvious as poverty. The designer must remind us all of a deep interdependence, and in doing so the flux can sound more like a cadence to life and less like chaos.

---

66 Charles Dickens, A Christmas Carol, 2003, Penguin, UK

Earlier I underlined the designer's role in society driven design in making conversations, though the use of dialogic and subjunctive speech and the employment of curiosity and empathy. In doing so - and by shaping better value exchanges and rituals - the designer is able to develop better conversational skills, making collaborators more likely to understand each other and less likely to judge one another. Communicating with honesty and integrity - however difficult - produces curiosity which begets, empathy which begets compassion, which affects our behaviour.

Dickens reminded Scrooge, that his interdependence was buried beneath his separate thinking - and by revealing this truth through his past, present and future, Scrooge could make better conversations across all his old and new relationships.

Our future is the sum of our past and present, and whilst our past cannot be changed, it must be understood accurately. Through Manet's mirror we are able to give ourselves over to a reflective process that enables a healthy understanding of our past. Enabling us to determine what changes need to be made to our present in order to arrive at a future version that is more accountable and interdependent.

Dan Hill's, *Dark Matter and Trojan Horses*[67], delves even further in providing us as designers with an embodied understanding of how we should be making these conversations. Firstly by viewing our profession of design as a practice and not a set of tools. Before we make anything, we are making conversations and the building of conversations requires the depth of a practice. Tools are by no means adequate to affect the change that we wish to see across our society, tools belong inside a tool kit.

Secondly, Hill highlights the difference between a deficit model and an asset one. Consultancies rarely have skin in the game. For the socially driven designer, understanding one's own values and purpose define the skin in the game to approach a conversation.

---

[67] Dan Hill, Dark Matter and Trojan horses, 2012, Strelka Press

Thirdly, the field of design thinking, is solely limited to Chronos units of measurements, and thus with the lack of Kairos, is deprived of meaningful connections. Design thinking lacks the vision to detect the dark matter that exists within a phenomenon. The dark matter that is revealed through a refractive process, one that takes place across nuanced conversations, and importantly one that needs to be embedded with care.

The designer should be aware that design thinking is a proxy for a first aid kit, a kit that can contain a set of tools to explore a problem with deficit thinking over a short time frame. A first aid kit is not a doctor and as such, no matter how clever we are, we cannot 'design think' our way out of poverty or re-offending. We are interdependent and as designers we must choose to embody our practice to act, making conversations that promote alliances. Alliances that even amidst the flux, can begin to produce a portfolio of micro interventions that will sustain us, doing more than merely surviving, but actually thriving.

The greater the uncertainty, the greater the potential for interdependence and subsequently the greater the alliances. Big changes can create stronger connections amongst us, deeper relationships that lead to antifragile networks - and complex alliances. We can start right now by being brave and exploring our own failure, not critically or with judgement, but lovingly, with compassion, encouraging ourselves to adapt and in doing so, adapt together.

Heraclitus noted that everything is in flux[68] and, as designers, we can respond to this by deepening our interdependence and designing stronger conversations and spaces in our understanding of each other. The safe and enabling environments we need to cultivate are the skills found in the fabric of our relationships: our love, tolerance and compassion.

Slowing down our lives with a refractive process to see failure more clearly; reminding ourselves, like Dickens' writing reminded us, that what we seek, we already have, (it's just likely to be buried under a lot

68 Heraclitus, On Nature, 2010, Kessinger Publishing, UK

of separate thinking). Adapting, communicating and being accountable to one another because we all inhabit this small planet and breathe the same air. Heraclitus, Van Humboldt and Dickens remind us, we were never disconnected in the first place.

By embracing our interdependence, like the Pando in Utah, we are able to champion alliances amidst flux, indeed the greater the chaos, the deeper the interdependence and the more beautiful the harmony. Life...always finds a way and with it, interdependently, we can design better ways of being human.

I believe in making things, making them well and making them together. My experience is that when we do this, things are revealed to us about who we are. These revelations provides us with the opportunity, to make change. Society driven design: improving us in the process and improving society by design.

Throughout his brilliant book, *AntiFragile*[69], Taleb illustrates - much like Heraclitus did - that change is the only predictable thing about nature, indeed change is so predictable in that it will always happen; Taleb likens this to a strategic growth approach within financial markets. For growth to occur there needs to be a set of market reactions that are built on change. Therefore, markets that mimic the volatility of nature are potentially making themselves stronger. Taleb continues to highlight three institutional approaches created to mitigate the volatility of change. *Fragile* approaches, a situation whereby the institution does not take any measure against market volatility and thus after any sudden economic downturn the institution becomes susceptible to going under. *Robust* approaches on the other hand are characterised by institutions who do build measures to mitigate the risk of a chaotic market and when that moment arrives are able to withstand the storm. Whilst *Robust* approaches fare better than *Fragile* ones, if a second or third wave of market volatility were to emerge, eventually the contingency resources would be depleted. An *AntiFragile* approach is one defined by institutions who are positively

---

[69] Nicolas Nassim Taleb, AntiFragile, 2012, Random House

depending on chaos and market volatility to occur in order to grow. Perhaps you can recall recent economic disasters, and in doing so you might recall certain institutions that emerged stronger for the process.[70]

How then, can we as designers seeking social change employ an altogether more positive antifragilie model to our micro initiatives? Antifragility cannot be sought without understanding the dark matter, indeed for the model to work financially an intricate understanding of markets are required, so too then for social change. An understanding that needs to include not just the known information but the embodied information too. A liquid understanding. An understanding that would only make sense by sacrificing time, both Chronos and Kairos. An understanding that requires the designer to make known their purpose and skin in the game, allowing for trust to be built. The perfect vehicle to hold all these activities is a conversation. One that connects with a diverse group of people across the phenomena. Collaborative conversations can also provide change in of themselves.

Certainly within my work across the criminal justice system and homelessness, I can testify to the power of collaboration as a genuine cohesive force for positive behaviour. Being involved in collaborative activities supports the development of enhanced competencies that can unlock positive social networks. Collaboration can be regarded as an example of active citizenship, enabling collaborators to enjoy a clearer path in accessing public services and resources. Finally I have witnessed collaboration enhance a range of existing services in prison and across probation too.

Collaboration in its most interdependent and diverse format can facilitate antifragility, and to this end, aids greater understanding across society through discussion and discourse, which can provide the space for change.

---

[70] Shorting the Sub Prime Market, 2007-2008, https://www.investopedia.com/articles/investing/020115/big-short-explained.asp

Creativity

In the early 1800's Ruskin, wrote: "all progress came at the expense of human welfare and the welfare of the environment.[71]" He believed that industrial innovation was able to move freely because it had very limited (if any) accountability, to the point that all innovation would arrive at the cost of societies overall wellbeing and the sustainability of the planet.

In ameliorating this state of affairs, Ruskin believed that we should be designing together, in a more harmonious manner, with nature. Laying the foundations for what we now know today as the National Trust was a way of seeking direct harmony with nature. The working men's art colleges, were also Ruskin's attempts to promote further harmonious ameliorations, where he married the knowledge of nature with self awareness through the art of creativity.

The working men's art colleges became creative learning spaces for men who were never afforded the opportunity of formal education. Instead of replicating school Ruskin was keen to provide a more aspirational approach to learning. He believed that to spend time in nature, observing it and drawing it, was a route to better understanding self, or put another way, we begin to see ourselves more clearly when viewed through the lens of nature. This was Ruskin's own Delphi maxim: *know thy self*. By studying the intricacies of nature, Ruskin believed the intricacies of humanity and ourselves would be revealed to the artist.

In an attempt to slow down innovation by attaching accountably, Ruskin demonstrated what innovation and accountability could look like by choosing to focus on areas of our society that rarely received any profile. He was able to bring accountability due to the status he enjoyed and his skin in the game. Often lecturing at the Royal Academy of Arts one day and travelling to the working men's art colleges the next, society began to notice this work, people began to share, thoughts, ideas, creativity, indeed conversations across space time and culture.

---

[71] John Ruskin, Unto This Last, 1860, Cornhill Magazine Publications

The depression in 1930's America presented some of the hardest economic times known to U.S. society. President Roosevelt, like Ruskin, recognised that attention must be paid. That the economy affects more than employment, but wellbeing, relationships and cultural fabric. Just like Ruskin who saw creativity as a vehicle for change, President Roosevelt commissioned an army of artists[72] to inspire a nation of hurting people. In this sense, creativity can be viewed as an act of care and wellbeing. Both Ruskin and President Roosevelt bore witness to the power of art and design as a contributor to social change, they were willing to leverage their status and sacrifice time and power in facilitating these life changing conversations across space, time and culture.

Principles for Collaboration
Un-designing Power
We have already discussed the value for embedding as a means of being able to action Kairos and Chronos. In doing so, we are able to develop a liquid understanding as well as revealing the speed, scope and scale of the phenomena we are exploring.

Dan Hill likens the art of embedding to a specific position within football, the role of the Trequartista, the Number 10.

A unique position in football, the Number 10 operates within the system but not necessarily of the system, playing a different game to everyone else on their team. Whilst most players are attacking or defensive in nature, the Number 10 is rather unique, in as much as they are doing both but in an unconventional manner. The number 10 is always seeking to exploit space. Master footballers like Xavi, Scholes, and Kroos would operate in that role, building space but not like an architect, more like the surveyor role we discussed earlier in changing the architecture of conversations. In a footballing sense the number 10 would be flattening the topography by making space where previously there was none. Pursuing one thing, the creation of space in support of others, whilst everyone else is exploring another - attacking or defending.

---

[72] President Franklin D. Roosevelt, 1933 The Public Works of Art Project

One of the roles the designer needs to occupy is that of the number 10 - not looking to 'do' but more concerned with the work in supporting the work. Dan Hill encourages the designer to explore the dark matter, however in doing so, the designer doesn't just understand the dark matter but learns to operate within it and around it, magically developing space, flattening the social topography - where once there were barriers, now they are understood and can be navigated if not removed..

Richard Sennet also explores the art of embedding through examining the role of the diplomat, referring first to the specific conditions before exploring the nuanced activities that live within the field of diplomacy. The diplomat undertakes a role that requires an understanding of cultures, customs and rituals - these are all different to one's own culture, which is familiar and often understood tacitly. In this sense the diplomat's understanding is semi solid. Explicit knowledge - solid, may not provide the internal social agility required when attending an evening soirée for example. In order to demonstrate a natural comprehension of culture, the diplomat must have an instinctive understanding of cultures to avoid a mechanical response. Therefore in learning new cultures, customs and rituals the diplomat must make the understanding explicit - solid, before they can make it embodied, tacit and thus semi solid.

Knowing the culture, the diplomat is then able to communicate different messages with varying degrees of urgency to intended recipients. Diplomacy contains many roles, each with distinctive skills, we are going to explore two; the envoy and the ambassador.

An envoy enjoys complete authority to represent the state, in the delivery of both difficult news and resolution of conflict, there is an immediacy to their work, operating in Chronos time. An accomplished envoy may possess the skills and understanding of value exchanges to resolve disagreements. The best envoys are able to be dispatched safe in the knowledge that their skill would ensure the most delicate of situations would be handled smoothly. In more chaotic scenarios envoys may be sought to resolve disagreements.

Envoys have a dynamic quality, but also require the deeper understanding of the dark matter that may cloak a nations customs and rituals. A masterful envoy is able to determine where subtlety is unnecessary, sometimes the skill to deliver a frank message with no ambiguity is what's required. The expert envoy knows the many different ways of delivering the same message in order to achieve the desired set of outcomes.

An ambassador, is a role that requires representation in a foreign land. This assignment demands a far deeper understanding of a countries culture and customs and thus an embedding process far superior to that of an envoy. The ambassador requires the vision of the number 10, in order to view both their own governments perspective, whilst demonstrating an enhanced knowledge of their resident state and the space in between. Being in a country, but not of a country, the ambassador is required to know the cultures and everyday customs but to maintain the ability of operating in a different way to others when appropriate or necessary. Different to the envoy, the ambassador sacrifices their time by learning the deep customs and rituals, whilst an envoy may only be expected to possess a general knowledge of several countries customs. An ambassador operates on Kairos time, building long-form relationships.

We have explored the role of the designer as a number 10 in football, operating with a different purpose but still within the system. We have also viewed the role of the designer as a diplomat, both as an envoy, often engaged in more dynamic assignments and as an ambassador, offering a more delicate approach across value exchanges and communication.

These examples provide us with a more spacious view of the designer, enabling us to observe the role of the designer, as Trequartista and as a diplomat. These are important proxies to evoke as we explore the hidden challenge of power within society driven design.

Imagine a local council, through a series of stakeholder engagement workshops, has concluded that their community faces many barriers to education. Through ongoing conversations with those passionate about change, it has been established that the community needs a new library. The council deploys a budget and creates a brief - inviting many organisations to tender their proposals - quite a few do. Ultimately the local council selects a wining bid by commissioning a human centred consultancy to deliver the project. The first workshop session takes place where members of the local community are invited to co-create the design of the new library.

Collaboration in the sense of socially driven design cannot happen if those we are seeking to collaborate with have not been involved in designing the brief. This is not a rejection of stakeholder involvement or indeed of the co-creative approach, however it is an illustration in the difficulty to detect power struggles even when the intentions are to do good.

Power must be reapportioned so that those who have been invited to collaborate have an active stake in deciding what it is they are actually collaborating towards. In the library example, power was hidden within the brief - in this sense whoever creates the brief, holds the power - however in different scenarios the power can be hidden amongst other behaviours or structures; perhaps the agenda, the physical architecture of the meeting room, or the social architecture of the workshop.

Power disguises itself in all manner of costumes and it is the skill of the society driven designer to identify where power is concealed as quickly as possible in order to un-design it and re-distribute it as successfully as possible. The diplomat and the Trequartista are often wrestling power from one base to another, they are able to do so with craft and precision. When working in UK prisons, we identified power hiding in all manner of places and as a result collaborated with the prisoners and staff in un-designing power where possible and working around it when we had to.

We identified power within the traditional classroom environment that triggered trauma for many of the men. Almost 50% of the 86,000 people in prison did not complete mainstream education.[73] (In the UK, Education is compulsory for all children between the ages of 5 to 16). The classroom setting would evoke memories of failure; calling to mind a teacher figure with judgement and anger looming over the younger version of themselves. Undesigning power in this instance was literally moving the tables and chairs and transforming the classroom into a professional studio.

We also identified, power hiding in the act of suppressing identity and the subsequent deployment of anonymity - exchanging a given name for a prison number. Un-designing the power of anonymity resulted in the creation of individual business cards for each learner. In presenting these cards we also designed a ritual of status, contributing toward the building of a safe and enabling environment.

Re-establishing Agency
The entry ticket for collaboration is agency. However, if someone hasn't grown up being modelled choice, how are they feasibly going to be able to exercise choice? Ensuring a wide and diverse range of stakeholders are around the table does not ensure a co-creation workshop will take place. Agency must never be taken for granted when exploring society driven design.

Choice is a luxury.

Being able to choose what clothes to wear, what to eat for dinner, what neighbourhood to live in or what industry to work in are choices that will possess a threshold of limitations for everyone. For some however, these choices can be very slim if a choice at all. Our choices are limited by a range of criteria such as economics or networks for example.

---

73 https://www.justiceinspectorates.gov.uk/hmiprisons/chief-inspectors-blog/chief-inspectors-blog-whats-going-wrong-with-education-in-prisons/

In the early days of setting up a homeless charity in London's most affluent borough of Kensington and Chelsea, (which was attracting the highest number of homeless travellers) the kitchen team, all of whom were securely housed - and who had all experienced homelessness - argued the case for having vegan options, halal options and kosher options all to supplement the standard meat and vegetarian options on offer every week.

We spent the next few weeks asking the guests what they wanted and I reported back to the kitchen team that 'everyone was happy with the existing meat and vegetarian options.' The team were unmoved by my feedback, and continued - rather passionately - to make the case for the wider meal options. I remained unconvinced, partly because no guest had ever asked for it and because I just couldn't envisage it. However, I knew the embodied knowledge of my team was dynamic and determined.

The team were absolutely right and we never stopped providing a range of dietary options from that day on. My team inherently knew that choice was important. Choice reminds us we are human. When I caught up with guests after our wider provisions, they happily told me how much better the experience was now they had a range of dietary options to choose from. What was fascinating, was that a few months earlier I had asked almost all the guests whether they wanted more choice and they said no. The agency to imagine a different way of doing anything should not be taken for granted. We need to design the spaces that provide a pathway back to re-establishing agency. For the homeless charity, a pathway for re-establishing agency was ensuring our staff and volunteer base included people who had experienced homelessness.

Choice reminds us we are human.

Choice of meal options at our shelter drop-in, London - 2011

Providing aspirational choice alongside community education, Chennai, India - 2009

Attempting to usher a collaborative space within the first six months of visiting prisons proved to be much harder than I could have ever imagined. In order to establish agency, I wanted to build a collaborative space, but in order to collaborate we need a history of trust, but then again to trust requires an experience of collaboration, (in some way), but to collaborate we need trust…so we have arrived at a paradox.

We cannot conjure up trust where it has been absent, yet collaboration becomes meaningless without trust. As designers, however, we have the advantage of understanding the power of creativity as a force for good. We explored earlier how Ruskin used creativity throughout the early 1800's when teaching working miners how to draw at his working men's art colleges. He believed passionately that draughtsmanship would act as a new language by which people could understand themselves better.

As designers we can encourage agency through a creative practice. I was able to break the trust-collaboration paradox in prisons by designing creative practices to inspire agency. Something as simple as asking the men to design an icebreaker gave us a license to 'make' something together, whilst also developing micro steps of trust in the process. Designing conversations does not always have to be through the vehicle of words, sometimes conversations can be through visual communication. Before we explored the icebreaker task, the men were unable to imagine or visualise the kind of innovation they needed. Similar to the guests at the drop in, who wanted choice but were unable to articulate it. In developing creative practices for the purpose of encouraging agency, the designer must create the space for choice, and in doing so, build trust through collaboration. Proxies for creativity can become effective ways of circumnavigating the trust-collaboration paradox.

Collaboration is a diminishing art.

Spending a lifetime working for one company is almost unheard of, so much so my M.A. students refer to that scenario as a fairytale.

My father worked for one company and many of my parents peers experienced the same. Today, few people are able to stay in the same company for more than six or seven years, organisations do not appear to be approaching long term hires in the same way as before - and as a result we are losing the skills of long-form collaboration.

As the skills for working together fade the nature of work becomes more task based. Project based work is often framed by achieving short to mid term pre-established goals or targets. We simply do not have the time to devote to the mastery of long term collaborative skills. The craft of the master diplomat will always fall outside the purview of short term project groups. Meaningful collaboration has become such a rare activity and as a result our work has become team orientated, declarative, dialectic and sympathetic.

Teamwork differs from collaboration, its dimensions focus more around tolerance than understanding. Teams are able to operate at speed, dealing with facts and clearly marking out the defined objectives - a didactic approach. As we explored earlier, collaboration does not blossom with declarative speech, indeed the collaborative spirit yearns for subjunctive conversations where ambiguity can be deployed, across space and time, allowing for questions and reflection.

When design is void of real collaboration it is in danger of becoming sympathetic, not empathic - and we run the risk of designing services as opioids - more of the same services *for* people or worse still, services applied *to* people.

I have highlighted how the changing environment of work has deskilled us. The fast vanishing skills of meaningful collaboration signify that working with people who are different to us, has become an oddity. Modern work is short circuiting meaningful relationships. The time and purpose that used to further the crucible of collaboration has become eroded. Society driven design must rediscover, through conversations across space, time and culture, the craft of collaboration in order to re-establish agency and choice.

Travel

Honestly reflecting on my decade of embedding across homelessness, led me to believe I probably did more harm than good. A factor in this reflection was my inability to provide the guests of the charity with the freedom to meaningfully travel outside of our initiative.

What I failed to establish were the portable skills to engage with different and essential environments. Instead of empowering our guests with the skills to successfully pass through into new situations, we made our drop-in an opiate. Our guests became dependent on our services and we in turn were dependent on them turning up to benefit from the services. Development became problematic and without wishing to be in this situation, we had arrived at a space where maintaining the status quo became our core work, but our aspirations were to cultivate change.

It's very difficult to live in one world and breathe in another.

When I started collaborating in prisons, I was keen to avoid making that same mistake again. Freedom to travel, is the concept that equips people to move from one place to a range of others. Freedom to travel is an essential element of society driven design, without establishing freedom to travel we run the risk of creating dependent non developmental initiatives. Once we are able to establish an initiative that provides a safe and enabling environment how might we create a portable version that lives within the person?

When we make things together, we can make change. This is important and due to our present iterations of work, this doesn't happen naturally. Making things together is a phenomena that is happening less and less. Therefore as designers, when we create the space for collaboration we must be switched on to the effect that collaborating will have on the individuals. When we make things together, not only do we make things better, but we make ourselves open to change. It is my belief that the more we collaborate, the more freedom to travel we are facilitating and the more accepting we become of others.

The more we all collaborate the more we all become better equipped for navigating society.

InHouse is not just a record label that works with people who have left prison, it is an educational provider within prison. InHouse is not just an initiative designed for prisoners, but it has been developed by prisoners and with prisoners. InHouse Records has been deigned within the dark matter that lives in between the systems. Dark matter revealed by conversations with prisoners, officers, governors and probation practitioners. Everyone involved has skin in the game and thus, a vested interest in the outcome. InHouse's antifragility is born from designing conversations that understood the divergent value exchanges, needs and wants of all the stakeholders, and sought to create the space for all to 'make' something special by un-designing power, establishing agency and facilitating the freedom to travel.

Government and the Private Sector
For the socially driven designer to meaningfully contribute toward conversations of change, we would do well to familiarise ourselves with a liquid understanding of the relationships between business, government and social change. Whilst capturing a history of public sector, private sector and social change would be a multi volume book in of itself, I am keen to pick out a few areas of interest for the practice of the socially driven designer.

We will be exploring the birth of Corporate Social Responsibility, its aims and objectives and adoption. In addition we will be looking at the role of the state in identifying social needs, and the ability to effectively meet these needs. Finally we will be investigating how the introduction of brands provided the space for consumer power. By exploring all these conversations across space, time and culture we will begin to identify the opportunities for a different kind of collaborative vehicle, one that can house the principles we have discussed earlier in this movement and legitimise these conversations.

Corporate Social Responsibility

What is Corporate Social Responsibility, (CSR)? As there are no legal requirements for a company to possess a CSR policy, many question its value all together.

In the 17th century, the Dutch and English developed chartered trading corporations called Joint Stock companies - a departure from the business operating model of the Guilds.

Those who owned stock in theses chartered trading organisation, were not the employees, who sought fixed payment for their labour, but shareholders, who were able to trade their stock and increase their personal profit. Enshrined in the legally binding nature of all Joint Stock companies was their requirement to provide a public benefit after the payment of employees and profiteering of the shareholders.

The definition of public benefit was loosely interpreted as shareholders benefit, as many Joint Stock companies chose to build and maintain their own gentleman's club which they believed provided a benefit to some echelons of the public, namely those who could afford the membership fees. One of the most famous of these Joint Stock companies was the British & Dutch East India Company.[74]

By the mid 1700's even more freedom to barter and exchange was provided to shareholders, as the government gradually began minimising any interference with business - unfettered access to make money, allowing corporations to do whatever the shareholders wanted.[75] The hunger for greater economic growth coupled with Adam Smith's[76] desire for free trade, paved the way for Joint Stock companies to become known as corporations.

---

[74] Royal African Company, Records, UK National Archives, 1672-1750, http://discovery.nationalarchives.gov.uk/results/r?_q=T70

[75] Smith A, The Wealth of Nations, Book 1, Chapter 2, Division of Labour 1776

[76] Smith A, The Wealth of Nations, Book 1, Chapter 2, Division of Labour 1776

These modern corporations, identical in many ways to Joint Stock companies, except not needing to provide any public benefit, were desperate for capital. The more money, the more industrial goods were purchased, the greater productivity. Shareholders generated more funds by selling the certainty of economic growth - profit became king at all costs. The access to economic growth, through a free trade that was unregulated by the government and with the power of industrialisation, created a perfect opportunity for the corporation to establish legitimacy.

In 1886 the supreme court of the United States of America ruled in the Santa Clara Case[77], that a commercial organisation could enjoy the same rights as an individual - a corporation could legally be viewed as a person. The Corporation was born, free to trade, free of delivering any public benefit and able to operate with the same rights and freedoms as an individual.

At the same time Karl Marx was arguing against unregulated trade. He explained "that the capitalist mode of production deprives workers from being the directors of their own action, being dictated by the capitalists, who own and manage the means of production and withdraw the maximum surplus value from the workers.[78]" Marx viewed the free trade, as free only for the shareholders.

Many Christian philanthropists shared a similar sense of caution. The Protestant work ethic [79]- hard work, frugality, moral goodness - although waning, was still partially evident in Britain in the 1860's, even though the Puritans, who were the foremost exponents of the ethic, had left for the shores of America almost 300 year earlier, possibly as a response to Luther's reformation thesis, or perhaps because they felt England was exhibiting loose morals.

---

[77] https://tile.loc.gov/storage-services/service/ll/usrep/usrep118/usrep118394/usrep118394.pdf

[78] Marx, K,, Economic and Philosophic Manuscripts of Karl Marx 1844

[79] Ryken, L,, Worldly Saints: The Puritans As They Really Were. 2010 Harper Collins

Had the puritans stuck around until the 1860's they would have witnessed an England where unfettered trade resulted in child labour. Children as young as four were employed in production factories and mines, working long hours in dangerous, often fatal conditions, managed by adults - many of whom would be drunk whilst overseeing life threatening working environments.

Someone who was keen to address the lack of social accountability was John Cadbury.[80] He and his family were anti-slavery activists and campaigned for abolition, by 1824 Cadbury opened a grocery store, although a Quaker, he was driven by the same Protestant work ethic of hard work and moral good. Cadbury had hoped that selling drinking chocolate would be an alternative beverage to alcohol. Many families were finding themselves in increasingly tough situations as many husbands would spend their weeks wages in the pub on pay day. Concerned that alcoholism led to poverty, Cadbury devoted himself to leveraging this new power of capitalism for social good. He offered society an alternative to the ale house, drinking chocolate emporiums charged a fraction of the amount and delivered husbands back to their families sober and wages in tact.

When Cadbury's sons took over in 1861, they continued to steer profits towards social good, demonstrated by their desire to create low cost homes for their workers, situated in a beautiful and healthy environment. Bourneville village, known as the factory in the garden provided a community swimming pool and featured the first recorded evidence of health care for staff. John Cadbury's son, George said, 'If each man could have his own house, a large garden to cultivate and healthy surroundings - then, I thought, there will be for them, a better opportunity of a happy family life.[81]"

George Cadbury provided one tenth of the Bourneville Estate to be used as parks, recreation grounds and open space and upon visiting Cadbury's former home in Woodbroke, I felt privileged to have read

[80] John Cadbury https://www.cadbury.co.uk/the-story

[81] George Cadbury, 1878 https://www.cadbury.co.uk/about/history/our-story/

the original draft documents and polices enshrining such innovative ideas as *pensions*, and *college educations* for the local community.[82]

Unfortunately examples of early Capitalism birthing corporations who chose to act with moral accountability are rare. *The Gospel of Wealth* [83] article, written by Carnegie - of Steel fame - was published in 1889, in it he encouraged the wealthy to give to the poor, like Carnegie himself did. However these represent outliers and not the mainstream. Indeed by the beginning of the 20th century the 'work ethic' had no place in business as society and culture entered into a new era. Capitalism was now completely free and many corporations exploited this - government interference long gone and the lingering outdated moral code seemingly retired.

Primary beneficiaries of this complete freedom were modern corporations such as Ford and Standard Oil. Replacing the moral code with a profit code - the race to the base. A race to save costs and increase shareholder profits - always in pursuit of the cheapest material, always looking to exploit the labourer, seeking the weakest labour laws in any given country or state to pay the least amount possible.

By the early 20th century, investors were the dominant banking institutions of London and Paris, who had invested heavily in U.S. Railroads, further intensifying a dependency on fossil fuels. As U.S. Railroads expanded, so did the shape of America, laying new tracks that linked previously isolated areas with new markets. With the rise of commercial farming, ranching, and mining, the U.S. birthed a super connected national marketplace.

American steel production rose to surpass the combined totals of Britain, Germany and France, whilst the banks of London and Paris poured investment money into the railroads through the American financial market, which was centred in New York's Wall Street.

---

[82] Dellheim C, The Creation of a Company Culture: Cadburys, 1861-1931

[83] Carnegie A, The Gospel of Wealth, 1901

The process of economic concentration and growth had extended into most branches of U.S. industry, and a few large corporations, called 'trusts', began to dominate in steel, oil, sugar, meat, and farm machinery.

A government who cannot understand public need, cannot create the goods to counter social deprivation. As soon as new machinery became available to replace any given work force, the race to the base would quicken - exploit the weakest, pay the least, make the most. Internationally recognised French Economist Thomas Pickety[84] wrote on the inequality of America in the Gilded Age, stating that America was growing further and further away from its original pioneering idea - the return on capital outpaced the growth of the economy as a whole, a dynamic which drives inequality.

By 1949 President Truman required capitalism to deliver development. The U.S. possibly felt threatened by the growth of Communism - and Lenin's rise to power in Russia, who themselves had become a world super power, providing the template for Marxist-Leninist governments in Eastern Europe and parts of Asia. Truman pressed the concept that international development would make significant improvements to underdeveloped areas, and Capitalism would become the engine for development. After almost 200 years of no moral requirements, Capitalism needed to be seen as a force for good.

Less than a decade later, Harvard scholar and economist Kenneth Galbraith[85], echoes Pickety and goes as far as to say that Smith's unregulated free trade is not suited to post World War II America, explaining that private sector wealth comes at the expense of a poor general public.

If Capitalism was to be seen as a force for good domestically and internationally then fundamental changes to the economics of

----

84 Pickety T, Capital, 2014, Harvard University Press

85 Galbraith K, The Affluent Society, 1958

Capitalism needed to take place. These changes did not take place, in fact no fundamental changes took place. Instead a bolt on was created and in 1953 Howard Bowen[86] introduced the term Corporate Social Responsibility. CSR was the solution by which Capitalism would become a force for good and in part help promote the notion that international development could carve a pathway out of poverty.

Bowen believed CSR would allow businesses to make a positive contribution to society, trusting that the same free markets that yielded economic growth could generate corporate benevolence. Porter and Kramer, social scientists, explored the trends of CSR, throughout the 1960's with a genuine belief that Capitalism and CSR would have a huge impact on poverty. When this did not materialise in the expected manner, during the 1970's the emphasis was shifted onto NGO's to make the difference with the financial support of corporates.

The landmark moment for CSR arrived in 1989 when ice cream corporates, Ben & Jerry's, produced the worlds first ever CSR report looking to bridge the role of shareholder and stakeholder by presenting an accountability to citizens of their actions; and a desire to make a wider impact, that operated as extra curricular to their practice. Four years later Body Shop began their 'Trade not Aid' campaign with the objective of, "creating trade to help people in the developing countries to utilise their resources in meeting their own needs[87]"; they had started a paper factory in Nepal employing 37 people producing bags, notebooks and scented drawer liners.

Interestingly by the 1990's with the effective fall of Communism, the need to promote capitalism had somewhat waned. Today, seventy years after Bowen launched the term Corporate Social Responsibility, the world suffers unprecedented levels of inequality and poverty. Inequality that recognises 20% of Americans earning less than 50% of

----

86 Bowen H, Social Responsibilities of the Businessman, 1953

87 Porter & Kramer 2011 Greenpeace, "The Ages and Stages of CSR", CSR International Paper Series, No. 3, 2011

the national median income. A global poverty that recognises 9.6% of the world's population are still living on less than $1.90 per day. Poverty and inequality that are paralleled with the findings from the Credit Suisse report: the world's wealthiest 10% owning 89% of all global assets.[88]

CSR was not a legal requirement. The corporation could choose to ignore CSR, in the same way many corporations chose to ignore the work ethic or the *Gospel of Wealth*[89]. A fading political placebo that used to promote development through becoming an affluent society. Both Pikkety and Galbraith recommended fundamental structural changes take place to Capitalism in order to drive down inequality - and whilst Bowen was evidently committed to the 'concept' of CSR, the lack of any legal obligation translated in a 'take it or leave it' offer.

In her critically acclaimed book, *No Logo*[90], Naomi Klein charts the marketing sea-change that would gift CSR a new lease of life. Klein recounts how the world of 1960's marketing became the world of 1980's branding. A change in approach - from adverting products to promoting a lifestyle associated with a master brand. The 'lifestyle' - for consumer facing brands - would swiftly become part of a corporate identity.

Computer corporation Apple's "think different[91]" approach to computing and sports wear giant Nike's "just do it,[92]" built strong images of 'lifestyle' around their respective product offering. The identities (or brands) that were created by corporates needed to be believable, but above all, they needed to be aspirational.

---

[88] Credit Suisse The Global Wealth Report 2016 https://www.credit-suisse.com/us/en/about-us/research/research-institute/news-and-videos/articles/news-and-expertise/2016/11/en/the-global-wealth-report-2016.html

[89] Carnegie A, The Gospel of Wealth, 1901

[90] Naomi Klein, No Logo, 1999, Picador, UK

[91] Apple, Think Different, 1997 - 2002 https://en.wikipedia.org/wiki/Think_different

[92] Nike, Just Do It, 1988 - 1998 https://en.wikipedia.org/wiki/Just_Do_It

The notion of CSR offered a layer of realism that could fit the aspiration of a brand. Creating an association between a company's wide range of products and the aspirational values of the brand. While individual products may have their own identities, it is the master-brand that contributes to the consumer's belief that the product is different compared to all others in its class. "Think different", is therefore not just an Apple slogan, but an invitation to a lifestyle that is presented as smart, youthful, connected, in control and less complicated. Historically, Apple have encountered a poor perception regarding their CSR - with their longterm Chinese manufacturing partner FoxConn[93] - coming under severe scrutiny for their working conditions and low pay. Eighteen attempted suicides, and fourteen suicides in 2010, caused one hundred and fifty staff members, to complain about the working conditions by threatening to commit mass-suicide. The adoption of CSR as a means of covering up less favourable practices can create a greenwashing exercise, but equally could ruin the legitimacy of a brand if the deception were to become public knowledge.

Both master-branding and greenwashing are examples of how CSR is leveraged as building the profile of the brand without actually providing any genuine social benefit. Rather like the Joint Stock's providing Gentlemen's Clubs as their public benefit.

The Latin phrase: *nemo judex in causa sua*, translated means no-one should be a judge in his own cause. It is a principle of natural justice that no person can judge a case in which they have an interest. Justice must be rooted in confidence and that confidence is destroyed when people are left thinking that the judge was biased. CSR, is not a legal requirement and thus, left to the discretion of a corporation to engage or not. However, even if a corporation chooses to have a CSR programme, ultimately they are judging themselves - producing their own report, or commissioning a report that they will sign off - or not.

_____

93 Life and Death in Apple's forbidden city, Brian Merchant, 2017, The Observer

Conversations Across Government

Today the modern corporation has much more rigour and compliance to adhere to than the Joint Stock of the past, however one legal requirement that has remained consistent has been taxation. What then of corporate taxation as a vehicle for ensuring Capitalism becomes a force for good? How are taxes directed towards the needs of the public.

Marc Wuyts, author and oxford scholar, defined public need as forms of deprivation, which become identified as problems in the public sphere: problems requiring public action. Public need arises from tensions and conflicts set up in society by economic and social deprivation. It is defined by political processes and changes with the transforming aspect of deprivation in society. Public need, therefore, is not just an identifiable 'thing', a feature of people's lives. Rather public need is complex, like the dark matter that lives in between systems and behaviour: it springs from social and economic deprivation, but is filtered through political processes which reflect tensions and conflicts in society - some call these tensions *wicked problems*[94].

Governments deploy funds available through taxation to meet the societal needs through the creation of public goods, delivered through non-market institutions, in a process called, public provisioning. The provisioning facilitates amongst other goods: public health and the education system, through state led provisioning which is funded by compulsory taxation. Public provisioning in the United Kingdom is absolutely dependent on a buoyant economy, allowing the populace to contribute via taxation to the economic governance of the country.

The UK private sector, can offer the exact same public goods, with an exclusivity. Seen more obviously in private health care and private schooling. The interdependency, therefore, on the private sector and government is evident. The private sector also provides household utilities, which is chargeable to the public.

---

[94] Witter and Webb, 1973 https://www.sympoetic.net/Managing_Complexity/complexity_files/1973 Rittel and Webber Wicked Problems.pdf

Where public action begins to reach the areas of abstract and extreme poverty in the UK, is where public provisioning creates public goods for those on the fringes of society. Pioneered by the great Nye Bevan in the early part of the 20th century, the Welfare State, was designed to assist the integration of those who had become marginalised, to become active participants within society once more.

How good is the government at identifying the nuanced public needs? Wuyts argues that, 'needs' spring from public and economic deprivation, however its conduit is through political processes. There is an assumption here, that firstly the public need, has a robust enough political process that surrounds it, which is free from corruption and can locally and, or, nationally facilitate this, 'need' being acknowledged and remedied. Secondly, there is an assumption that if there is a shortfall in the political process, that civil society can intervene to make up the difference.

What becomes clear, is that even with a robust government, social deprivation needs more than a political process, and the benefits system to make a difference. However what is unclear, is the twilight space that CSR and the Third Sector operate - whatever the Public Sector cannot or will not do is left for others to pick and choose. However no one is checking to see who picks up what or if there are issues that remain untouched, needs that remain unmet. There is no care being exercised.

We are unclear about the ability to detect needs in the first place, or even if detected that we may have the resources or competencies to identify remedies or perhaps still if political corruption might cloud the whole process. The society driven designer, must operate above CSR, and around it and beside it. The society driven designer should be operating outside of the Third Sector, within the gaps, embedding in the dark matter. The society driven designer must operate with and without the government. Attention must be paid.

Conversations across the Private Sector

We have explored the difficulties of engagement with CSR due to its non-legal and optional nature. There have been many attempts to coax the private sector into embracing CSR and by studying a few of these attempts we can begin to form a liquid understanding of the successful, (and unsuccessful) approaches. The socially driven designer must be aware of the conversations that have taken place between businesses and those seeking a fairer society - the conversations that have taken place over space, time and culture.

In 1979 Archie Carroll[95] took Howard Bowen's words from 1953, that called on businesses to adopt an altruistic vision and created a CSR Pyramid. This was a way of helping the private sector to understand their role in creating a better society. The pyramid featured standard practice business behaviours at the foundation (economic stability and legal compliance), and suggested that social responsibility is at the apex for any modern business. Carroll put forward the notion that corporates will want to do the right thing, when it comes to ensuring that neither people nor the planet are harmed in the production or manufacturing, delivery, promotion or consumption of their goods or services. In terms of CSR the pyramid made sense, it just didn't make a tangible difference.

In 1994, John Elkington[96], founder of British consultancy SustainAbility, continued on the themes set out by Carroll's pyramid by fusing corporate language with CSR values and revealed the 'Triple Bottom Line'. Elkington stated that companies should be preparing three different sets of accounts. The traditional business set of accounts, known as the bottom line - this approach is also in keeping with Carroll's first pyramid tier of economic responsibility.

[95] https://www.sciencedirect.com/science/article/abs/pii/000768139190005G

[96] https://www.johnelkington.com/archive/TBL-elkington-chapter.pdf

Second, Elkington suggests a people account needs to be constructed – a measure of how socially responsible an organisation has been throughout its operations over the course of a financial year to all humans. Elkington is keen to stress the responsibility that employers have to staff, consumers, third party staff, communities who live close to their factories, all people who are affected by a company's activities. Unfortunately, the clock speed of change in terms of labour rights, tends to operate slowly and often actioned only in the wake of a disaster. The thousands of deaths on the U.S. railroads preceded Labour Unions. The Rana Plaza disaster in 2013, killing over 1,135 people preceded a meaningful shift in manufacturing across the fashion industry.

The final bottom line is that of a company's planet account—this is a measure of how environmentally responsible a company has been over the course of a financial year. The Triple Bottom Line, represents a change from previous CSR nudges as it was one of the first to position environmental impact alongside financial and ethical concerns.

For many organisations who were tethered to fossil fuels, the thought of a planet account was difficult to imagine, indeed for many organisations in general, a planet account proved difficult to grasp.

The picture of the whole Earth as seen from space, known as the 'Blue Marble' represented the first photograph in which Earth is in full view. The picture was taken on December 7, 1972, as the Apollo 17 crew left Earth's orbit for the Moon. Imagery plays a huge part in understanding a phenomena, our ability to view the Earth outside from ourselves is still a modern one, it is important therefore that the designer recognises that use of symbols and pictures, especially in the process of affecting transformation.

Elkington's triple bottom line (TBL), represented some progress from Bowen's call for altruism forty years earlier, but like Carroll's pyramid, lacked teeth to implement any consequences.

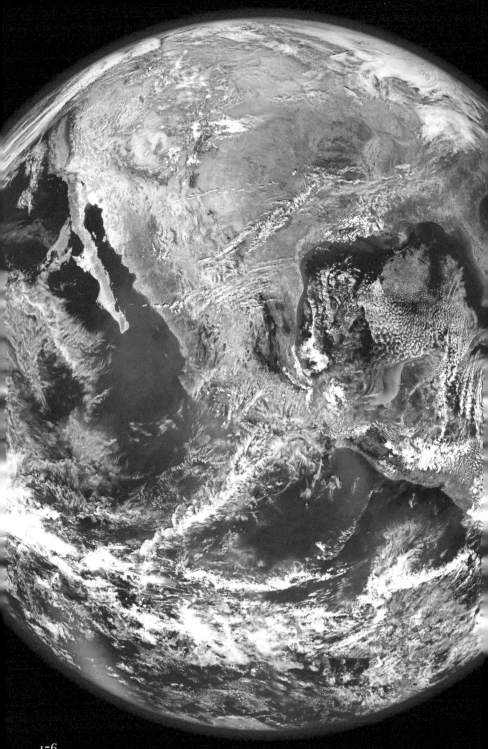

Five years after Elkington's triple bottom line Naomi Klein released her book, *No Logo*[97]. Klein revealed a clear trail of deeds and misdeeds starting from the products that consumers purchased, all the way up to the brands that consumers trusted. The lack of jobs and choice in countries with weak governance, was being exploited by the brands in countries with strong governance - resulting in the creation of sweatshops, bonded labour and the unethical and unsustainable globalisation movement.

Bowen, Caroll and Elkington were wrapped up in conversations to nudge the private sector into a moral compliance, whereas Klein took the story to the people. She made the consumers aware in no uncertain terms that the crimes taking place half way round the world were actually being triggered by the t-shirts being sold on the local high street. She invited a new set of stakeholders to the conversation - the public. In doing so, she made the public aware of their own involvement in the process. We are complicit.

In the previous section we identified the challenges that the public sector has in identifying public need, resourcing public need and designing remedies to challenge it. Similarly, how are businesses equipped to identify the issues they are creating? Who is responsible for picking up the bill for the true cost of business behaviour?

International economist Raj Patel, in his 2009 book, *The Value of Nothing*, explored how we might measure the true cost of produced goods or services, if we are not measuring the negative impact that these goods or services are creating.

To Naomi Klein's point, are we measuring the cost to the lives of the people who are exploited in sweatshops, or measuring the cost to the planet from irresponsible environmental practices?

---

[97] Naomi Klein, No Logo, 1999, Picador, UK

Patel attempts to capture the true cost of a cheeseburger produced by an internationally recognised franchise. He considers the cost of the CO_2 caused by cattle, the cost of the packaging which can't be recycled, the fossil fuel to generate the power for the factories and the exploitation of desperate migrant workers willing to take on unenviable roles. Patel arrives at a real cheeseburger cost of circa £1000. Who is picking up the hidden cost? One part of the world continues to develop, but in doing so it's transforming a significant part of the rest of the world into a backwater.

Recalling President Truman's inaugural speech[98] and the promise of Capitalism to provide development, perhaps the opposite is true? Capitalism - through the race for the cheapest and its dependency on fossil fuels - has contributed to greater poverty and disparity not rectified it.

Through discussing the narrative of CSR, from Bowen to Elkington we are able to view the gradual erosion of philanthropic responsibilities. Bowen believed that CSR had to begin with corporate altruism and Carroll placed philanthropy at the apex of the CSR pyramid. Elkington omitted philanthropic responsibility altogether, focusing on tangibles like ethical and environmental behaviour, of which Patel highlights are not even being accounted accurately.

Perhaps what all the approaches from Bowen to Elkington lacked was the deployment of a language that could be easily understood by all. In that sense Klein wrote in a language of endings, one that invited engagement in a bid to change business practices.

The Social License
We explored the interior journey of the designer within the first movement - the need to define design and the importance of the

---

[98] President H Truman, Inaugural Address, January 20th 1949, https://www.trumanlibrary.gov/library/public-papers/19/inaugural-address

designer defining their own values. Earlier in this movement we explored the exterior ingredients for socially driven design - the principles for collaboration and the attributes of conversations. We have also looked at some of the systemic frameworks provided by the public and private sector.

In the final chapter I will make a case for how the interior values, the exterior principles and infrastructure can be housed within a new collaborative process - The Social License, legitimising our conversations.

The Social License was a 19th century practice of legitimisation, that sought to provide equity and authenticity. The process enabled neighbourhoods to evaluate the potential future practice of businesses that may infringe on a communities wellbeing. Businesses would seek the approval of a community before they were able to work, in effect, a business would obtain a Social License to carry out its proposed works. As with CSR however, the Social License was never made a legal requirement, thus remained an optional process that failed to deliver meaningful change.

The Social License Re-imagined
Society Driven Design is a conversation, that requires the designer to craft meaningful and diverse conversations. The development of these conversations need the designer to become expert in value exchanges and rituals. The designer leans into their liquid understanding for wider vocabulary that can not just support conversations but determine the speed, scope and scale by which to approach a phenomena. However keeping in mind the principles for collaboration, creating a safe space that un-designs power and re-establishes agency becomes a necessity. The Social Licence is new proposal for collaboration. Once naturally exercised by Cadbury, the use of the Social License provides a vehicle for conversations that can span across space, time and culture yet still be validated and recognised. The Social License provides the interdependence that was prominent in the ancient Guilds and can point towards a more equitable way of measuring progress through network understanding.

The art of collaboration, transitioning from endings to beginnings is a much more proactive iteration of the Social License. The License becomes the primary artefact of collaboration, and initiatives that are derived from the establishment of the License, automatically have legitimacy.

The designer can shape how businesses are born without setting out to design businesses, but by establishing a Social License; meaningful collaborations that transition from endings to beginnings and beyond. Transitioning to a new language that can provide awareness of self, promote agency and enshrine the resources to chart a virtuous route towards a golden future.

The Social License can only exist through meaningful collaboration, guaranteeing that whatever we ultimately design together will inherently have the DNA of the communities that birthed it. The Social License will offer the designer the forum to craft conversations of transition with subjunctive and dialogic skills and always with empathy. Conversations of complexity featuring diversity, adaptation and interdependence that will naturally become part of what is created by The Social License, because the collaborators are diverse, interdependent and adaptive. Aspiration will naturally be part of whatever is created because those designing are those engaging. A conversation provides co-ordinates of a starting point, not just of a person but of a community who are committed through engagement and increased appetite to see situations changed.

The Social License can provide the designer with the opportunity to shape better transitions and conclude better outcomes than our current penny pinching, globalised and independent approaches offer.

Better transitions allow for meaningful collaborations, enshrining the space for a portfolio of micro interventions, designed outside of time and across societal boundaries, captured within the collaborative vehicle of the modern Social License.

Many designers cannot afford to work years on a project. The Social License makes this possible. Conversations across space, time and culture can be recognised, valued and validated.

Design can do better.

The Social License in Practice
The Social License is a safe and enabling collaborative approach, where future License holders are invited into conversations about their neighbourhoods, facilitated by the socially driven designer. There are no agendas, or briefs to work to.

I will be demonstrating four key areas where I believe the Social License holds more truck than traditional co-creation workshops or co-design approaches - greater legitimacy, transparent motivations, sustainable communities and delivery of long term value exchanges.

The Legitimacy of the Social License
I have the privilege of seeing many Masters Design students annually prepare to graduate as they begin to explore a working life within design. Some of my students will leave the Royal College of Art wanting to make a difference and I have no doubt that they will. All the students are keen on building a career. These two objectives can operate mutually as well as exclusively, building a career can also mean making a difference but actually it's ok if they are separate. We do not have to work in social change to make a difference.

Sacrifice
The point of the Social License is that it is accessible for all, and this must include the socially driven designer who will be hosting the conversations. The Social License cannot have a pre-determined agenda or brief as that would usurp power from the group, to that end it must be agenda-less. In the very first movement of the book I shared the importance of the interior journey for the designer.

To make anything, we must first be clear what it is we are willing to give up. The Social License requires a sacrifice of time, Chronos time, and Kairos time, to build meaningful relationships. The sacrifice of the designer is a viable demonstration of skin in the game and legitimacy, which is a helpful contributor to building trust and equally breaks the trust-collaboration paradox.

Identifying Public Need

From the four layers of a functioning society; public sector, private sector, third sector and community, it is only the latter which is *not* an institution. Citizens are in danger therefore, of being dependent on institutions for change. The four layers of societal function rely on three institutions that have all the policy making agency. However as we have discussed in the previous section the ability for these institutions to identify public need is problematic for a number of reasons. We are unclear about the ability of the state to detect the needs in the first place, or even if detected that we may have the resources or competencies to identify remedies that can make a difference or maybe the threat that political corruption might take place and bury the issues completely. Equally the private sector cannot be their own judge in shaping their own CSR reports, especially if the hidden ethical and environmental concerns will never be revealed.

The Social License provides agency for citizens that can hold accountable the three institutions of a functioning society through collaborative conversations that provide the space for all to take part. In doing so, we create the safe and enabling environments for true needs to be revealed and the actual costs of epistemological error. InHouse Records was able to identify a range of needs that went above and beyond the headline of recidivism, however this would not have been possible without the agenda-less time to host conversations with the License holders in and outside prison.

As we discussed earlier the whatever Public Sector cannot or will not do in terms of public needs is left for others to pick and choose.

The **Social License** provides an **official validation** for all designers to legitimately host long form conversations across space, time and culture.

The License offers the community an iterative **living document** of their conversational development and equips the wider stakeholder group to **de-risk** initiatives of social change.

However no one is checking to see who picks up what or if there are issues that remain untouched. The Social License can be a legitimate way of not only identifying needs but also delivering care through recognition and action.

Motivation
In the first movement of the book we discussed the importance of defining the motivations of the socially driven designer. Hosting conversations across a diverse group of stakeholders the designer as diplomat can begin to glimpse the motivations of all the collaborators. Understanding the diverse motivations of all the collaborators illuminated a pathway for the development of InHouse Records. The long-form nature of the Social License allows for motivations to gradually come into focus in a way that time bound interviews or workshops simply could not capture.

What if someone's wealth could be lost as easily as catching a cold? What would we do differently to ensure we created a vaccine against poverty? Would we find a solution to poverty as swiftly as we developed the Covid-19 vaccine? The Social License not only provides the long-form space to identify motivations but the collaborative environment to build modern value exchanges where winning becomes a universal feature for all License holders.

Organisational Structures
Sennet underlines the importance of a community organiser, in his book, *Together*, by bluntly observing that, Labour Union organisers turned out to be poor community organisers. He would continue to point out that self organising groups would find it difficult to shape effective dialogue.

Hosting conversations across space, time and culture requires the socially driven designer to adopt a nuanced position within the process. Existing organisational structures find it difficult to provide a space that can be open and vague in the pursuit of equitable collaboration. Hierarchical structures can be problematic due to the disempowering nature that the leader may be inadvertently triggering.

Similarly, self organising collaborative structures can lack direction and focus leading to chaos. The Social License requires the host to occupy the role of a diplomat - designing conversations that are neither hierarchal nor self organising.

The Sustainability of the Social License
The Social License that championed InHouse Records, is still operational today. A group of License holders exploring conversations across space, time and culture. Conversations that have nurtured some brilliant artefacts, like InHouse Records but also conversations that have informed existing initiatives like the fantastic work of Catch22 - exploring meaningful ways of connecting with people after being released from prison. Indeed the work of Grand Avenues - providing place based probation, has also been informed by the License holders that delivered InHouse

License holders are connected for more than a workshop or a series of interviews, indeed the Social License formed around criminal justice has been operating for almost a decade. The sustainability of the conversation begets the confidence that change can take place. License holders come from all areas of the phenomena, unlike the CSR frameworks that were developed for the business leader, and more like Naomi Klein's *No Logo* that introduced a much wider range of stakeholder to the conversation. The Social License can provide the safe and enabling environment for all who occupy the space to engage.

Networks
When we make things together, we not only make them better, but it's better for us. As Ruskin pointed out in the early 1800's, governing systems were catering for individuals, where once they were communicating to the household. Even though we know we rely on a community, we still insist on measuring the individual. The designer must approach how we measure by re-ordering and refracting.

We are linked to one another in myriad ways, through families, neighbourhoods, schools, workplaces, friends, friends of friends and possibly even enemies. All the people we are connected to have their own connections, who, likewise, know and interact with their own groups, and so on. We all have networks, connecting us to individuals and various groups. Our networks are powerful, they contribute to our social well-being and lead to the exchange of ideas - just like the genius of Ancient Rome. Our networks can dictate our career trajectory and even act as an early indicator of our earning potential.

Networks can increase our life expectancy and can even be a contributing factor in how quickly we are able to travel to a hospital in an emergency. Networks can predict the likelihood of re-offending. Networks, as Ruskin alluded to in the *Law of Help*, can be life giving.

A network is a group of interconnected actors - these actors could be people, organisations, systems, or things. Networks can vary in their nature and operation, communicating different information depending on the actors involved and their relationships. Networks operate at different levels, scope and context.

Most importantly however, networks provide us with the opportunity to explore the nature and behaviour of an actor derived from their function or place within a larger whole. Within medicine, network theory enabled scientists to track the spread of a disease viewing the larger picture - like tracking Covid-19 with a global or regional context. Within ethnography, network theory provided a way of conceptualising family relationships and migratory patterns from tribal villages to cities.

Networks differ from other information based models of organisation, like markets or hierarchy for a number of critical reasons.

Interdependence
Networks are unique because the actors are interdependent. Markets contain actors that are independent of each other, allowing for goals to be achieved through buying and selling. The network *interdependence* of actors means that no single actor can order others to act in a certain way - and no actor is *so* dependent on others that they must obey others.

Networks differ from hierarchies, in which the authority of one actor enables them to demand the compliance of others. Human networks demonstrate our interdependence; interdependence that was inherent in Ancient Rome, or the Medieval Guilds, communities in Chennai or InHouse Records; we are all reliant on each other to progress.

We cannot achieve our goals unless we co-operate with others.

Ruskin's 1837 *Law of Help* states, "The collaboration of all things across everywhere in order to sustain life.99" Ruskin saw in nature the essential networks that need to be maintained in order to sustain life. He argued that such a law should be applied to human development. CSR provides models that rely on independent transactions observed in isolation, however if we want to achieve a corporate responsibility for *social* development, our model should be planted firmly within *society* and not within the heart of the corporation.

Value Exchanges
Market models are based on property and ownership rights and rely on price to regulate, whereas hierarchical frameworks are based on employment relationships relying on authority to regulate. Networks, however, are based on *value exchanges* between the actors - and rely on trust. These value exchanges are formed through rituals and developed over meaningful conversations.

Markets resolve conflicts through bargaining and where that fails, the courts, and hierarchies use rules and commands. Networks use tactful negotiations and diplomacy.

Collaboration
A final difference might be culture: markets operate on a competitive culture, hierarchies instantiate a culture of subordination, whereas networks encourage a culture of reciprocity - the alliances that Ruskin spoke of.

---

99 John Ruskin, Unto This Last, 1860, Cornhill Magazine Publications

Networks are based on value exchanges and rely on trust, networks resolve conflict through negations and diplomacy. Actors cannot obtain their aims unless they co-operate with others, interdependence, therefore is a unique and distinctive feature of networks over other organising models.

Our social networks do not just highlight our inherent interdependence, they also improve our health. In a recent report published by the National Library of Medicine[100], we learn that people with access to diverse groups of social relationships live longer and have less cognitive decline with ageing, greater resistance to infectious disease and better prognoses when facing chronic life-threatening illnesses. The more diverse our networks, the healthier we become. We have known that having a more diverse network in business improves our career trajectory, which has a direct impact on our earning potential. The more diverse our networks, the more successful our careers are likely to become.

The Value of the Social License

Beyond the initiatives that the Social License may deliver, the value of the Social License becomes the process. It is the process that nurtures skills for both the License holder in navigating new networks and nurturing agency, as well as the socially driven designer in forming a wider language of endings and transitions. I began one Social License formed across the criminal justice system and one across homelessness both have been significant sources of liquid understanding over the last twenty years.

Learning

In the spirit of the Medieval Guilds, the Social License seeks to house the collaborative nature of learning and making. Together we explore a craft to conversations that can lead to the development of artefacts or initiatives of real value, however the ongoing liquid understanding evokes the trust that parents would demonstrate to the guilds.

---

[100] https://pubmed.ncbi.nlm.nih.gov/20161087/#:~:text=Persons with more types of,facing chronic life-threatening illnesses

A trust that these spaces could advance something so much more than that of an extractive research interview, but of choice based architecture - the opportunity to make a difference for self and to play a part in making a difference for others too.

The Social License provides the environment for 'genius' in the sense of the Ancient Roman term. A collective and collaborative space where the idea is not the goal but the fluid conversation, one where nuanced value exchanges have been crafted and rituals observed and made to further aspiration. The 'genius' that requires ambiguity to thrive, the dialogic and subjunctive speech to ensure the conversation is not limited by expectations but connected through empathy, kindness and compassion.

Time
Whether Chronos or Kairos, the value of the Social License is that it provides an abundance of time. The time for people to develop the skills to make weak connections, not just the necessary skills for deep relationships, but the skills to befriend the 'other', the skills that modern work no longer nourishes as short form employment facilitates didactic and declarative speech.

We need long-form spaces that house aspirations, challenges, hopes and fears. The kind of spaces where someone can talk of endings and beginnings. The kind of spaces where behaviour can be modelled and a new way of seeing life can be imagined.

Design must inhabit these spaces.

The Social License allows all designers to sacrifice their time, and host conversations with a diverse group of license holders across space, time and culture. No agenda, developing agency, un-designing power and forming liquid understanding.

The Social License promotes meaningful change.

BEGINNINGS

Beginnings

Humans make things.
We have an innate desire to build. To create. To make.
Making things reminds us we are human.

These days it feels like we are encouraged to consume things rather than make anything. I do not believe we were made to consume. For the society driven designer to be able to make things with others, they need to make conversations that remind everyone we are makers, not consumers. There is a symbiotic relationship between the designer defining their values and the quality of the conversations that are designed. When we are able to make sense of things well, we can make things better. When we make things, we 'want' less. The maker in us all needs to be freed.

Making is a beginning. Across this movement I will be sharing the extraordinary story of InHouse Records, connecting the liquid understanding with the transitional collaboration in order to nurture the space for change. InHouse Records provides a real life example of beginning something in challenging circumstances.

This movement consists of four parts; *understanding and insights -* where I will share past and present sense making coupled with primary insights. *Theories and assumptions -* across which I will be examining existing theories applied to our liquid understanding and as a result shaping some primary assumptions. In the third section I will share the *conditions for change* that have been formed and informed by understanding, insights, theories and assumptions. Finally, the conditions for change provide the blueprint for *designing meaning.*

Beginnings Part One
Understanding and Insights

Making sense of the Past
Can I contribute to reducing recidivism?

This was the question I asked of myself before exploring the application of design within the criminal justice system. In truth, I had no idea if I could contribute anything of value, but I was willing to embed within a system and begin developing a 'liquid understanding' of the space which started with ongoing conversations and the formation of what was to become a Social License in the criminal justice system. Before we design anything, we must design conversations, in the case of InHouse, these conversations took place across the justice system, spanning across areas of space, time and culture. Conversations that first led to an understanding of the past, 'how on earth did we end up here?'

Britain has held a profound relationship with punishment ever since the Romans left in 380AD. From hanging criminals to flogging them and from beheadings to placing those deemed guilty in the stocks, punishment became a fluent public language; a deterrent to transgressive behaviour.

Punishment, in part, had become a tool shaped by the wealthy in order to protect their wealth. 'The Bloody Code[101]' of the 19th century reinforces this ideal, as it featured over 200 crimes that were punishable by death including shoplifting, stealing sheep, cattle or horses and the theft of goods valued at twelve pence. Of course, it was natural for people to protect themselves and their property; however it is worth noting that the poor did not have such protection.

'The Bloody Code' also included the death penalty for crimes such as being in the company of foreigners for a month, or providing strong

---

[101] The Bloody Code, 1723, National Justice Museum https://www.nationaljusticemuseum.org.uk/museum/news/what-was-the-bloody-code

evidence of malice in a child aged 7-14, remarkably, taking another person's life was not always seen as a crime punishable by death.

However cruel and unjust, the consequences of punishment were clear, there could be no ambiguity; break the law and punishment will be exercised upon your body, and sometimes this would result in loss of life. In the 16th century, being homeless was viewed as a crime, as was being unemployed and no distinction was made between both those phenomena - they were classified as 'Sturdy Beggars'. In 1547 a bill was passed that subjected 'Sturdy Beggars' to the death penalty after their second offence. In effect, if they were caught more than once committing the crime of being homeless or unemployed they would hang. During the reign of King Henry VIII it is estimated by historians that around 72,000 people were executed.[102] Punishment was seen as acting out retribution and by making the punishment public, it could also act as a deterrent to the rest of society. Executions would perform the role of a 'grisly deterrent' for would be criminals, and serve to remind the rest of society that the law's far reaching power and might could not be escaped.

Public executions were less of a solemn affair and more like a macabre fete. Experienced entrepreneurs and entertainers would travel great distances in anticipation of selling their goods to a large audience, arriving hours before an execution, ready to set up their stalls.

The public's fascination with punishment was highlighted by the popularity of the, 'Execution Broadsides', a single sheet newspaper, featuring the gruesome details of the crimes committed by those who would be executed later that same day. The phenomena of the 'Execution Broadsides' was made possible due to the arrival of cheap printing in the 1500's, thanks to Gutenberg's revolutionary invention fifty years earlier.

If the details of the crime were vague and unknown to the reporter, the Broadside press would revert to simply making up their own stories, printing gory rumours about the crime in the absence of truth.

---

[102] John Stow, The Survey of London, Project Gutenberg 2013, originally written 1598

The press were creative in their methods to sell papers. The 'Execution Broadsides', were available to purchase near the gallows for a penny and in addition to text, The Broadsides would feature a woodcut illustration, often depicting a convict's final hours in jail before execution. The text accompanying each story of execution would follow the same format: a paragraph capturing the dark details of the crime, followed by a paragraph that contained a full and complete confession - often including a cautionary warning to anyone contemplating a life of crime.

The details of the crime (true or not) and the full confession (true or not) were seen as essential components in the construction of a deterrent. The public must not be afforded the space to doubt the power base of the law. Therefore, the Broadside were obligated to print a confession regardless if one was actually made or not (usually not). Doubt was allowed to creep into the minds of the audience on the rare occasion the guilty were allowed to scream their innocence en route to the gallows if the executioners team had forgotten to gag them.

Broadside traders would sell commemorative execution souvenirs, as well as pornographic material to appease the frenetic mob. These morbid days boosted the execution economy and even provided the space for ministers to deliver sermons against the backdrop of jugglers and jesters.

Eventually the Execution Broadsides were faded out, perhaps consumers didn't believe the stories that were printed; the crimes or the confessions. Fed up of reading made up stories about real people, it should come as no surprise that within a decade of the Broadsides fading out of circulation in the early 1800's, England birthed the first crime novel - now people could read gruesome made up stories about made up people. The broadside created a taste for gore and an appetite to know the criminal mind. Are we any less interested in crime fiction, drama or documentaries nowadays?

To make sense of punishment today, is to understand punishment from the past. In doing so we are able to see how the conversation across space, time and culture has thematically changed and how the society driven designer must be acutely aware of these thematic endings. Things end. We must become fluent in endings if we are to make sense of beginnings.

The first of these endings is that of capital punishment. The death penalty was suspended in 1965, just after the last execution in 1964, and then permanently abolished in 1970, ultimately it was made illegal in 1998. However, the ending of one thing is the beginning of another. Whilst executions ended, punishment did not. The vehicle for punishment was no longer death. Indeed justice stopped punishing the body as it began punishing the soul. The vehicle for punishment became a lack of liberty, for a duration to be determined by a court of law.

When the death penalty stopped so did the need to use machines to enforce capital punishment. Machines to punish the body were replaced with prison regimes. The gallows, the stocks and the chopping block were now obsolete. The vehicles used to deliver punishment became concrete and psychological. Prisons use of monotonous routine, restricting movement and removing freedom all have an impact on the human will and the designer exploring this space must be aware of these dimensions.

Finally the public execution put an end to the public witnessing any form of state punishment. The last public execution in Britain took place in 1867, meaning that for almost a 100 years afterwards, all executions were performed behind closed doors until the last execution in 1964. Once upon a time the publicity surrounding punishment was both a deterrent and a show of power, today punishment is not only private it's become anonymous. Where once the name of the guilty party about to be executed was printed alongside their confession for all to read, now the whereabouts of a prisoner is not public information and whilst the tabloids will still write about the crimes, the punishment takes place in private.
For the prisoner, this thematic shift has a profound impact on their identity, from once having a name to now being given a number.

Things end, and whilst punishment remains, the understanding of how it is commuted becomes of huge significance to the designer operating in this arena. Governments ended the practice of publicly punishing the body with machines by privately punishing the soul with monotonous routines.

What I learnt from these many conversations is that any collaboration must communicate through the language of the soul, because it is the soul that is being punished. I needed to use expressions of creativity to uncoil that which routines have distorted, and that I must provide the space for identity to reveal the anonymity of obscured self. This liquid understanding shaped the language I needed to adopt.

Before we design anything, we must design conversations.

Making sense of the Present

By observing the factors of speed, scope and scale and with the critical insights that helped us make sense of the past we were slowly able to make conversations, ones that became tangible. InHouse Records began by shifting the power and as we explored in the previous movement un-designing power is a fundamental principle of collaboration. Therefore by choosing to have no agenda or brief we were able to shape conversations that were led by the prisoners themselves. I have to be honest, these were not easy sessions at the beginning, can you imagine standing in front of a group of alpha men many of whom probably didn't want to be there, but equally were expecting something from me, only for me to say I had no agenda apart from hearing their ideas. It was tough. Making sense of the past helped, however what helped the most was reliability. I made it clear that I would be giving up my time for as long as they wanted me to come. It was strange at first to meet with no agenda but after a few weeks, it started to feel normal. Creating the space to host conversations, is a building block for creating the space for change to take place. This is why the Social License is more than a project.

These early ambiguous conversations revealed three primary insights, that coupled with the thematic changes of the past began to give the space to shape new conversations; theories and assumptions. These three insights also formed an integral aspect of the Social License that would enrich future initiatives beyond InHouse Records.

Focusing on what's strong, not what's wrong[103]

Many consultancies will adopt a deficit approach when presented with a challenge, identifying the problems, seeking out the gaps, focusing on what's wrong. A deficit approach to measuring the educational achievement of a prisoner will always find gaps in their learning, especially if that individual has experienced any kind of challenging circumstances. A deficit approach will invariably determine some kind of intervention to bridge the gap. In prison, this may practically look like the provision of low-skilled workplace training like industrial

---

[103] Cormac Russell, Asset Based Community Development, Rekindling Democracy, 2020 Cascade

cleaning or entry level construction - which may not suit or be aspirational to every prisoner.

An asset based approach requires the designer to look closely and identify where the opportunities are - and not where the problems are. Asset finding has a different approach to problem finding, where deficit relies on critique, asset based demands imagination; the skill of seeing something that is not yet visible. Focusing on what's strong acknowledges these inherent skills by re-visualising them through 'core competencies', such as communication, problem solving and leadership.

When seeking to host conversations across a phenomena, identifying the scope presents the opportunity for the designer to navigate the complexity of a moving landscape. Determining this Social License, I chose to define the scope by establishing those who were the most vulnerable to re-offending repeatedly. This resulted in collaborating with men who had found themselves in prison for drug related crimes. The scope provides the context for exploring change.

The conversations revealed the collaborators' embodied understanding of portion pricing, product, stock, supply and demand. These were known terms and methods - known for the wrong reasons - but known never-the-less. These methods are extremely transferable to business. An asset-based approach allows us to look closely and identify where the opportunities lie – not just the problems.

Viewing the core competencies of basic business as a desirable asset, which almost all of the men possessed, allowed us to create the first level of an educational programme - basic business. The reason we began at a level that was already known meant that almost all of the men would not start from an educational deficit but could actually start at an advanced position - skipping ahead to level two - basic business for the music industry.

Creating a starting platform whereby all the learners could immediately advance to the next level created profound results. Our learners were not starting an education journey in knowledge debt, which had been the norm their whole lives, but were commencing a programme where their skills, (not their crimes) were being recognised - and more than acknowledged, actually contributing to their studies. Enabling growth in confidence, acceptance and engagement from the get go. Within a few months of operation, InHouse Records' waiting list (the number of prisoners signing up to the programme) grew to over 300%. We were instantly popular and a significant factor had been our asset based approach defined by scope.

Focusing on *what's strong, not what's wrong* can help to make sense of someone's past by repurposing their future.

Non-linear interactive storytelling
If we want to bear witness to genuine development, we must create the space for prisoners to negotiate the terms of their own rehabilitation.

I was keen to ensure we did not replicate school where typical curriculums of study were often inflexible and didactic. I was also aware that re-establishing agency would contribute toward continued collaboration, so the desire to provide an education platform that supported choice based architecture was high. However it was only when my good friend Fillipo Sanzeni shared how sandbox design, known more formally as non-linear interactive storytelling or, open world gaming, deployed an everyday example of choice based architecture that could be repurposed for our conversation.

The learners at InHouse Records decide what they will learn, when they will learn and how they will learn it. They define the dimensions of their own learning and as they do so, we are on hand to ensure they are able to develop a realistic programme in order to achieve all that they have set out to achieve. In practice this may look like building a programme enabling someone to manage an artist in the music industry, or learning a programme that provides steps to becoming a producer, or learning to play a musical instrument and co-write with other artists. The pathways to study correlates to the roles that exist within the music industry, all the work is project based which makes setting timelines easier as well as ensuring engagement remains high.

All the course work leads to a goal: an album, a performance, a marketing campaign.

It is an important insight to establish, that rehabilitation only becomes possible when a person is given a choice or agency over their actions - if they are forced to sit and 'think about what they've done', the opportunity to exercise personal change becomes remote. Choice reminds us we are human; InHouse provided that space, as much as the chefs at the homeless shelter preparing a wider range of meal options did - thus allowing people to make choices and take control of their own actions.

The storytelling element captured within InHouse Records not only allowed for learners to make sense of their narrative, (revealing identity) but also created the space for dialogue - and more conversations across space, time and culture.

The vocabulary for the average prisoner is reduced to less than 1,200 words after being incarcerated for twelve months. Before we design anything, we are designing conversations. Non-linear learning or unstructured learning, naturally promotes curiosity, which leads to the ability of expressing feelings with a wider vocabulary. Cognitive articulation of self is paramount to mastering emotions and the more this growth can take place the more we see words being connected to feelings, and emotions begin to develop a vocabulary that helps regulate. Learning to express ourselves articulately leads to a desistance of violent behaviour. In the process of learning, everyone broadens their vocabulary as we seek new words to express the new phenomena we are experiencing. The carefully crafted design of InHouse Records, slowly and gently nurtures communication, verbally, non-verbally, visually and through written format all within the safe and enabling environment of a record label that provides the architecture of choice.

Continuum
The issue with projects is that they end. This is problematic for those who have a history of things ending badly.

InHouse seeks to model positive, healthy relationships through all our staff interactions but, especially through mentoring. Sustained mentoring creates the opportunity for learning positive coping mechanisms, and also stimulates the curiosity for structured learning. An example of this can be drawn from how we may get started at InHouse, by a learner building their own curriculum. The learner will start by charting a map of aspirations - there is no template to this map, for some they will draw a literal map identifying their starting position and where they would like to land post release. For others they may draw something more akin to a systems map and for others a mind map. There is no right way of drawing a map of aspiration, and perhaps that's the point, what matters is having a personal map that allows both the learner and the InHouse staff member to chart a pathway of learning. Providing consistency allows participants to nurture trust, competencies and technical skills. Through the process of developing InHouse within UK and USA prisons I discovered a truth, that people - in particular those in challenging circumstances - often have a bad relationship with relationships.

Things end.

Endings can occur due to a range of differing reasons, but one factor is undeniable, that many in prison will have experienced abruptly ended relationships, indeed many will have experienced relationships that ended by a primary caregiver walking away never to return.

As I began to realise the experience of, 'bad endings' suffered by our collaborators, it became imperative to ensure our collaborators could end their experience of InHouse positively.

To establish healthier exits from InHouse, I knew we couldn't exist as a project or charity, as both of these formats cannot even guarantee the terms of their own endings and additionally require a significant degree of someones time to be dedicated towards fund-raising.

Once I had shaken hands with my collaborators I couldn't create something that would end as soon as it had started. The last thing the men needed was someone parachuting into their lives, making promises and exiting stage left. They needed consistency.

We must learn to navigate better endings and the society driven designer, must adopt the skills of an envoy to develop a portfolio of fluency in endings. The beauty of how InHouse has been crafted, is that just like the curriculum, the learner is given the space to negotiate the terms of their own departure from InHouse. I wanted to be part of an initiative whereby the collaborators could decide how and when they wanted to end their relationship with InHouse.

Ending something well, provides the space for better beginnings. As designers we must provide the space for all to decide how and when they wish to begin and end their engagement. When learners graduate from InHouse - and are released from prison, they are invited to continue journeying with the label at various recording studios. These are spaces where music can be recorded and rehearsed, but also, studios represent more than just a place to make music they are seen as contact centres for fathers to meet their children, studios are an enabling space to work through benefit forms and housing applications and indeed studios are a place where probation officers can meet with our graduates. The journey with InHouse in the community can end whenever the graduate feels it's time to move on - and whilst ending is never final with InHouse, (as many graduates will come back for showcases), ending the frequency of the sessions and ending these well, is a significant step in managing relationships. InHouse Records isn't just designed in order for individuals to be better musicians, but also supports individuals to become better collaborators, better fathers and sons.

Continuum means an ever developing ever changing process over time, like the continuum of life long learning, or in a more nature based perspective, the continuum of the four seasons. I haven't found a better vehicle to incubate initiatives, such as InHouse Records, than 'not for profit' legal entities. Perhaps you can develop more nuanced entities for these continuums to operate. I never imagined society driven design would lead me to become a founder and to that point,

I have been designing myself out of these continuums consistently as the ending of my role, shouldn't be the ending of the continuum.

Beginnings Part Two
Theories and Assumptions

Across this chapter I will be sharing the evolution of two critical theories that support the understanding and insights from the previous chapter and by doing so fostering the creation of two assumptions. These assumptions are more akin to advanced conversational prototypes, ready to be tested and re-tested through dialogue.

Network Theory

We briefly discussed network theory in the previous movement - networks as a component of the Social License. Everyone has a social network - the people in our lives whom we share the most time with. Our ability to grow and maintain these networks depend on the kind of person we are. Whether we thrive by spending our time with a small circle of friends, or wether we flourish by connecting with a large group of acquaintances.

In developing InHouse Records we focused our attention on three specific archetypes that had been developed by Janice McCabe[104] - who writes extensively about the power of social networks. These archetypes are variations on ego nets or socio-grams - presenting a network from the viewpoint of the ego. It's worth noting that these archetypes should be seen as possible indicators to how people are able to make sense of themselves through others and, as with any theory, there are always flaws, exceptions and outliers.

Our first network archetype is called a, *tight knitter* and looks rather like a knotted ball of string. A typical *tight knitter* will have one close group of friends where almost everyone knows each other. The *tight*

---

[104] Janice McCabe, Connecting in College, 2016, Chicago University Press

knitter is significantly impacted by their friendship group. The best iteration of the group is one where everyone takes care of each other with emotional and practical support. My friends in Chennai are a good example of positive *tight knitters*, where everyone knows each other, everyone supports each other, and it's easy for everyone to balance time spent with each other, because everyone lives together. *Tight knit* networks do have a dark side however, and this can lead to the reinforcement of bad behaviour as well as potentially feeling suffocating. Almost all our collaborators from prison identified with being in a ball of string network. However unlike the folk of Chennai, their *tight knitters* have high potential to be toxic, prone to group think and reinforcing negative behaviour. No rehabilitative initiative can successfully operate unless they take into account network theory. Ball of string networks are very difficult to break out of.

The second archetype we studied is called a *compartmentaliser*, imagine these networks to look like a bow tie. A typical *compartmentaliser* spends their time between two separate groups of friends. Each group represents a triangle of a bow tie, with the *compartmentaliser* being the knot in the middle. Neither group are known to each other. Sometimes this can lead to nurturing different behaviours depending on which group the *compartmentaliser* is in. However the positives are that the *compartmentaliser* is able to turn to either group for valuable help and support and they can more easily avoid the reinforcement of bad behaviours by limiting their time with a particular group. However, *compartmentalisers* must learn how to balance their time and energy between both groups.

The third network archetype we explored is called a *sampler*. Imagine these networks to look like a daisy with plenty of petals. A *sampler* will have one to one relationships with multiple groups of friends who do not know each other. A *sampler* doesn't necessarily have one tight group of friends, instead they have friends from a range of different groups across their life. It is easy for a *sampler* to avoid the peer pressure of one group, because they are able to dip in and out of so many other groups. The drawbacks for a *sampler* however, is the potential to miss out on the cohesive support that may often be naturally found in close knit relationships. Instead of balancing time and energy between 'groups' of friends, the *sampler* does this with a handful of individual across their network, often their friends are not even known to each other. We knew we wanted to communicate through the language of the soul, and to do so utilising a non-linear interactive storytelling approach - providing choice. We also knew we needed to establish safe and enabling environments, where we could focus on what is strong, not just what is wrong - and we knew this needed to be wrapped up in a continuum. All of these insights led us to explore our first question; how can we provide the *transition* for individuals to move from a ball of string network to a *bow tie* network and possibly beyond?

Our challenge therefore was not to change the archetype, merely the networks they found themselves in- the *tight knitter* could still access a core group of friends but they could also access a different network too. Perhaps their core group of friends could be made up from two different networks like a bow tie, or actually they curate their own core group of friends into a daisy network. To achieve this outcome, we needed to identify *how* to navigate different networks and if that was possible we needed to understand what are the skills required to do so effectively?

Recovery Capital Theory
The phrase, 'recovery capital' was first published in research undertaken by Robert Granfield and William Cloud. Granfield and Cloud[105] were exploring the phenomena of addictions, specifically the differing affects the same addiction may have on different people. They were intrigued how it could be that one person, addicted to alcohol or drugs may still appear to function normally, even holding down their role as a CEO of an organisation for example - whilst another person, addicted to the same cocktail of opiates is unable to function at all, slowly losing their day to day operational capacity.

---

[105] https://pubmed.ncbi.nlm.nih.gov/19016174/

In pursuing this phenomena Granfield and Cloud revealed the variable presence of four different types of *capital* inherent in every human who might find themselves in the challenging circumstance of addiction. As with network theory, there are flaws and outliers with recovery capital, however holding the theory in a liquid understanding we were able to form a direction of travel for our prototypes. Human capital concerns itself with the acquisition of technical skills. These are skills that enable individuals to perform tasks or an entire scope of work that contributes to a job. These skills can be learnt at school through traditional qualifications or at the work place leaning a trade for example or perhaps modelled by parents and other family members through chores around the house like DIY, gardening, budgeting for food shops or cookery. Those who explore further education, a degree or a masters for instance, are increasing their human capital, as are those in long term employment. There are some jobs that provide minimal human capital because the skill may not be valued so much in society.

Social capital concerns itself with the skills that enables an individual to make and sustain all manner of relationships, but especially meaningful and intimate relationships. Social capital can be observed and learnt through peers, demonstrated by teachers or modelled by parents and family members. Our primary learning phase for the bulk of our social capital occurs at the earliest stages of life. As children it is through the development of self and other, that we are able to form alliances and share. These primary interactions provide the building blocks to form relationships of all types, from deep and meaningful to colleagues at work.

Cultural capital focuses on the growth of knowledge and the demonstration of that knowledge by the application across different frameworks; such as political, socio-economic, religious or the arts for example. The use of cultural capital helps us order and understand how certain parts of society work, and where the edges of politics connects with economics. Cultural capital is primarily learnt at school and university, modelled by peers, employers and parents but of course cultural capital runs throughout one's life. In practice cultural capital may facilitate a deeper understanding of business through understanding economic and political frameworks that might house Neo-Liberalism for example.

Economic capital focuses on the the earning potential of an individual, which can be derived by combining all three of the previous capitals together. However economic capital also concerns itself with an individual's financial modelling through such frameworks as credit ratings, or actual cash in the format of savings and income, or the lack of cash - debt.

An individual's recovery capital, is the sum of all four capitals. Amongst many other insights, Granfield and Cloud, were able to observe that those who possess large amounts of social capital are able to maintain some kind of daily functioning ability even when addicted. The more networks an individual is part of, the higher their social capital and thus, the higher their recovery capital.

Social capital, therefore, is an imperative asset of recovery capital, however even more significant for InHouse Records, social capital could be seen as a network passport, allowing an individual to develop the skills required to journey from a toxic network to a healthier one - social capital provides the *transition* to move from a ball of string network to a *bow tie* network.

How can we promote the growth of social capital to provide the *transition* for individuals to move freely from a ball of string network to a *bow tie* network and possibly beyond?

Language
Observing the lack of recovery capital amongst our collaborators, the next critical objective was to define the specific characteristics of social capital that could be applied to our continuum in order to transition from ball of string to *bow tie* networks.

We ordered and re-ordered our liquid understanding. Our collaborators in prison, had rarely been modelled the skills to foster and sustain healthy relationships - most had grown up either in care or without a primary care giver who had the capacity to model social capital. In addition, we knew that over 50% of those in prison were let down by the education system[106]. The growth of social capital occurs at the primary stages of our lives - our childhood - without frequent exposure to positive modelling of social capital, there is the risk that those in the most challenging circumstance will grow up to become social immigrants, on the fringes of social norms, on the edges of acceptance and belonging.

UK Prisons had become exponentially more violent over the years preceding InHouse Records[107], (between 2013 - 2017), coupled with the shocking realisation that the average UK prisoner will see their spoken vocabulary diminish to less than a thousand words after a year in prison, we began to see a correlation between social capital and violence.

Social capital consists of the skills that facilitate the making and sustaining of relationships, but those in prison have often experienced negative bonds with relationships - all things end. Positive iterations of networks are based on value exchanges that rely on trust, therefore we knew we had to shape win-win exchanges based on new rituals through collaboration.

Actors of a network cannot obtain their aims unless they cooperate with others though interdependence. Our challenge was to collectively find that which is aspirational amongst the prisoners in order to collaborate, whilst being able to do so in a language that speaks to the soul. For the soul is being punished and in speaking to the soul we needed to provide the space for identity, agency and choice. The choice to reflect in Manet's mirror and choose to travel to a different world, a *bow tie* world, where the possibility of hope can be a reality.

---

106 https://prisonerseducation.org.uk/2022/08/prison-education-undervalued-and-under-resourced/

107 https://prisonreformtrust.org.uk/wp-content/uploads/2023/06/prison_the_facts_2023.pdf

It became apparent that we had transitioned towards a profound convergence; all of our collaborating cohort spoke in a language void of vulnerability and thus generating meaning within a relationship became very difficult. This adapted language, empty of social capital, prevents accountability, agency and nuanced communication from breaking through - and without these, the scope for curiosity that begets empathy, that begets compassion is limited.

The adapted language grows to become impervious to change, minimal scope for integration and exploration - growing more and more armour plated the more time spent within a ball of string network. This is a harsh language that cannot grow and does not allow for play. A language that lives, like those who speak it, on the edges of our society, difficult to understand and the point of exit for many.

In my experience with the collaborators, rehabilitation has never been about becoming good (whatever that means) but about language becoming more meaningful. Perhaps it has always been about language - the harsh language of the execution broadsides from Medieval England. The cruel language of absent fathers, missing throughout a boy's life. The brutal language of the care system. The severe language of the punished soul. The barren language that cannot grow and the bleak language that does not allow play. Loss. A lack of conversation across space, time and culture.

A lack of conversation.

Meaning
Transitioning from reflection to refraction, it became obvious to us - not just what the components of social capital needed to be - but the engine for InHouse Records.

Meaning.

Our challenge was to re-establish meaning through words, "whereby the world to which a man belongs to, can become the world which belongs to man.[108]" Transitioning to a new language that can provide awareness of self, foster agency and enshrine the resources to chart a virtuous route towards a golden future. We approached meaning from two different perspectives, trust and core competencies. Our first challenge was to make language meaningful.

We knew that positive networks use value exchanges, trust and diplomacy to regulate, therefore our first perspective by which to explore meaning was trust. Our second perspective to approach meaning would be lead by our understanding of recovery capital and the core competencies that were absent in the social capital amongst our collaborators.

Beginnings Part Three
Conditions for Change

Testing the assumptions through conversations paved the way for developing a blueprint for change. By understanding our insights, theories and assumptions we were able to construct conditions for change; designing trust and respect. In doing so we established factors for the re-design of trust and respect.

Trust
In shaping the rituals, through creativity, we established an equilibrium for trust and collaboration, allowing us to break the paradox, and in doing so reveal the dark matter of the phenomena.

Once the paradox of trust and collaboration can be broken, the designer must explore ways to nurture the space for trust to be re-built meaningfully and collaboratively. Whilst almost impossible to design for because of the intangible nature of trust, we must focus on creating the conditions for trust.

---

[108] Rowan Williams, Edge of Words, 2014, Bloomsbury

Conditions for trust - Consistency

Without fail each prison I visited had a storage facility somewhere on site, that contained the artefacts of past projects that ended abruptly - half a drum kit from a charitable initiative that someone forgot to pick up a decade ago, a bass guitar missing two stings and a neck warped like a banana that was left behind as the initiative ended without an opportunity to return.

As our collaborative initiative began to grow, word of our creative progress spread across the prison leading to a prison officer inviting me to come and see their haul of musical instruments. A room full of discarded and unappreciated artefacts - I hadn't been prepared for feeling so overwhelmed. These forgotten instruments filled me with despondency; once upon a time that bass was held tightly by a prisoner, excited to be making sense of feelings that had been bottled up for their entire life. As the project ended so did their grip on those aspirations of self discovery.

When designing the conditions for trust, the designer must ensure consistency. It became apparent that whatever we intended to make together we needed to ensure its consistency. Nobody wants an infomercial host to parachute into their lives, promising hope, selling 'new' and disappearing unexpectedly, without warning, as swiftly as they arrived.

Our collaborators didn't need more people to let them down. The parent that left and never came back, the teacher caught in a system that didn't afford them the time to understand their challenges in a different way, the employer that didn't take the chance on them, when actually all they needed was a break, in order to break out of their ball of string network by being introduced to a new one.

Looking at that broken bass guitar I didn't want to be part of the same cycle of rejection. I knew we needed to build consistency. For InHouse Records to make a meaningful beginning, we needed to understand the endings of previous initiatives therefore the first condition for trust became consistency. The condition of consistency meant InHouse Records needed to guarantee the time of any staff that would support this initiative. We needed a sustained income, we could not function as a charity and thus *had* to be an enterprise, one that generated an income that could sustain itself. One that provided value to the prison network.

Conditions for trust - Frequency

Alongside consistency we needed to ensure the condition of frequency. I recall one afternoon in conversation with our collaborators, the dialogue focused on organisations that come into prison once a year for a few days. Here is an example where consistency exists but the frequency was terribly low.

Establishing a regular time with the men was essential, however the frequency of that time needed to be more than once a year. When exploring socially driven design, the designer is always accessing the world of care and designing for care is a craft that cannot be compressed. Establishing frequency for an initiative will require the designer to observe factors of speed, scope and scale, as well as highlighting the different value exchanges that have been informed through the conversations with the stakeholders.

We knew from our conversations that trust had been so deeply eroded amongst our cohort that daily frequency was essential for the rebuilding process to stand any chance of success. To that end, the flagship prison in which InHouse Records operates, HMP Elmley, has been amazing in allowing us to deliver InHouse Records every day of every week of every month since 2017.

The exceptional staff at HMP Elmley have made this possible. The necessity for meaningful conversations across space, time and culture becomes manifest when attempting to design the conditions of trust. These conversations have become embedded not just with the prisoners but with the prison staff in all the prisons we operate in. Governors and deputy governors, prisoners and prison officers, will all move on - as Heraclitus said: "everything is in flux[109]" - we are not building a fixed entity but a fluid conversation - one that can be visited

---

[109] Heraclitus, On Nature, 2010, Kessinger Publishing, UK

in continuum. Therefore we must always be ready to keep the conversation going all the time to allow for flux and change. The personnel will change, but the conversation remains fluid. Before we design anything, we are designing conversations, ones that outlast those who started them - The Social License.

Conditions for trust - Reliability
In determining the conditions of frequency and consistency we were able to establish a third condition: *reliability*. Simple messaging that InHouse Records was open for business every day, and then actually being open everyday, enabled InHouse to be dependable. In this sense the condition for reliability becomes a by-product of delivering promises, indeed every time we make a promise and are able to deliver upon that promise we are able to increase a condition of trust. The designer should be aware of the power in promise making - as the inability to deliver on a promise will encourage mistrust. With this in mind promises must be made carefully and through collaboration as we transition from endings to better beginnings. Reliability, certainly in the early stages required a sacrifice of my time, and it is inextricably linked to ensuring income, as reliability can only be guaranteed if we have staff that we know are reliable.

Respect
Our challenge was to define meaning through words; whereby the world to which a man belongs to, can become the world which belongs to man. In establishing frequency, consistency and reliability as conditions for trust we were able to deploy these conditions towards tangible dimensions - what, how often and when. By establishing the conditions for trust we were additionally able to build positive rituals through repetition.

Trust building was demonstrated through logistical messaging, however we also needed conditions for change that would foster interior growth and engagement. We touched on the theme of 'respect' in the first movement whilst exploring the internal journey of the designer and their relationship towards design. We also looked at the respect that the Guilds were able to amass - the parents that respected the Guilds enough to entrust their children's education to them. However respect plays a significant part in how an individual can progress in society.

Factors of respect - Achievement
Respect is earned by achievement, but this achievement has to be recognised by mainstream society in order for it to be regarded as valid. Society respects the individual that has made something of themselves, whether that is by studying or entrepreneurship or simply climbing up the career ladder. Achievements that are understood by society are celebrated by society. Achievements have to mean something to the collective, before the collective can validate the achievement of the individual.

Respect is a much harder condition by which to establish trust than that of frequency, consistency and reliability. The manner by which respect is earned makes it very difficult for society to respect prisoners or those who have been to prison. Indeed respect is equally difficult to obtain if someone is an outsider. For those on the edges of society, the messaging is clear, you do not belong and earning respect will be an uphill struggle.

Factors of respect - Self sufficiency
Respect is also earned by being self sufficient. Society will generally respect those who have never asked for help, indeed we admire the self made individual that is able to support themselves. For anyone growing up in challenging circumstances, it is almost impossible to gain respect associated through self sufficiency. Receiving statutory support, being in debt, or asking for housing benefit are all examples that place an individual outside the scope for gaining society's respect.

Factors of respect - Philanthropy

Finally, and probably most significantly, respect is earned by philanthropy. Society looks favourably on those who are not only self made and resourceful but especially those who can afford to help others. Achievement, independence and charity are the hallmarks for earning respect and the greatest of these three is philanthropy. For anyone currently experiencing challenging circumstances, the act of philanthropy may feel as realistic as time travel. Society does not respect you if you have not made anything of your life, or if you are not financially independent.

The designer must use expressions of creativity to uncoil that which regimes
distorted. Building the conditions for change with kindness and emp

Creative sessions of expression HMP

Beginnings Part Four
Designing Meaning

Prototyping, in the product design sense, may often result in model making in order to visualise the scale, ergonomics and feasibility of a design. In socially driven design, prototyping has similar purposes, however the model we are making will almost always begin with a series of conversations in order to ensure the collaborators can form and inform the shape of the proposed initiative.

As we spoke collectively about our factors of respect and conditions for change (prototyping), we began to see some clear ways in which we could re-design respect and nurture genuine conditions for change.

Re-designing Respect
How respect is earned requires un-designing. We must look for alternative ways of measuring achievements; by focusing on what's strong not what's wrong we are able to view a new possibility. Through InHouse Records we are able to recognise alternative forms of achievement. Our collaborative cohort all found themselves in prison for drug related crimes, therefore great care is taken to ensure we separate the skills from the actual criminal activity and its consequences, in doing so we are able to view achievement that would have normally remained invisible. By acknowledging alternative forms of achievement, we are able to provide a lens for the individual to re-imagine their past.

Earning respect by being self sufficient is problematic for many reasons; there is a presupposition that being dependent on one another is a bad thing. Somehow publicly we are encouraged to not rely on each other, as validation of self sufficiency leads to respect. However privately, society appears to have far less of an issue regarding dependency. Society respects the self sufficient and independent, separate thinking person. What confusing messages are we sending to people in our society? Be independent in public and interdependent in private.

Un-designing the respect gained by self sufficiency requires an understanding that we are *all* interdependent and that self sufficiency is a dangerous trait to measure as a mark of respect. We must create the space for those in challenging circumstances to be able to negotiate the terms of their own support, whatever that may be. We must demonstrate a reciprocal trust in the awarding of respect.

The term *blocking* often used in modern cinema actually has its origins in theatre and is a technique used, often by the director, in order to communicate to all the actors where they would need to stand on stage for particular scenes. The term is called blocking because the director would actually use small wooden blocks as proxies for the actors, placing the blocks on a scaled drawing of the stage whilst talking through everyones positioning in relation to the script, sound and lighting cues.

In cinema, *blocking* has similar connotations - the director places small blocks of wood on a piece of paper to suggest where the actors need to stand in relation to the multiple cameras that are positioned around the film set for any given scene. However the medium of film provides limitless floor space compared to the theatre stage, and as such *blocking* becomes more nuanced. The film director must determine the actors' movements, body positions, and body language in a scene. The blocking process involves working out the moving camera positions, the in-motion lighting design, the sound configuration and specific set design. A film director who didn't *block* would spend more time and money shooting the same scenes again and again.

One of the cinematic masters of *blocking* is multi Oscar winning director Steven Spielberg. From films such as *Close Encounters of the Third Kind*[110], to *Jaws*[111] and *Raiders of the Lost Ark*[112] - Spielberg masterfully uses the movement of the actors and cameras like a

[110] Steven Spielberg, Close Encounters of the Third Kind, 1977, Columbia Pictures, EMI Films

[111] Steven Spielberg, Jaws, 1975, Universal Pictures

[112] Steven Spielberg, Raiders of the Lost Ark, 1981, Paramount Pictures

cinematic tango, seamlessly in synch. In a recent interview Spielberg was asked to reveal the secret to his *blocking*. In an unexpected response Spielberg revealed he rarely *blocked* scenes himself, in fact, he trusted the actors get on with it.

For respect to be un-designed and re-designed with equity, including those in the most challenging circumstances, we need to find alternative ways of measuring achievement. In addition we must trust those in the most challenging circumstances to negotiate the terms of their own support. This trust must be freely given, with the understanding that with such trust comes the potential for agency, choice and opportunity. Spielberg's most successful films were blocked by his actors, the trust he showed them all in negotiating the terms of their own agency is a perfect proxy for how we should be looking to un-design respect.

At InHouse Records we trusted the collaborators to negotiate their own terms. In essence we asked them to metaphorically '*block*' their own scenes. Within the first week of the Covid-19 pandemic we explored this technique and trusted our collaborators, who then delivered something truly spectacular. Aux Magazine is the UK's only award winning music and cultural magazine designed by prisoners and those released from prison, exclusively for those currently in UK and USA prisons. A full-colour journal that provides articles on wellbeing, life after prison and progressive learning through cultural and musical cues.

For the first 12 months of the pandemic Aux Magazine was the only content exclusively designed for prisoners that was being delivered on a weekly basis to over half the UK prisons for free. We are still producing this award winning magazine having exceeded 70,000 copies.

At the homeless shelter in London we trusted the kitchen staff - all of whom had experienced homelessness themselves - to cook a range of different meal options and in successfully '*blocking*' their own scenes they were able to highlight that choice reminds us we are human.

Finally, we must de-couple philanthropy from being the only factor by which respect is earned through giving and supplement it with the giving of compassion and kindness. Viewed in this sense many people I have met in the most challenging situations have been able to show compassion or be kind - by being present, giving up their time, or providing their empathy through acts of kindness. Given the opportunity, we can all establish better ways of being human.

At InHouse Records we built trust across the dimensions of consistency, frequency, reliability and respect. We realised that the way respect was earned needed to be explored, un-designed and re-designed to make it attainable for all.

Re-designing Social Capital
Defining meaning through words because those words had become harsh and meaningless, became the supreme meta-narrative of InHouse Records - allowing us to make sense of it all, before we began to make something very special.

The convergence of two separate channels of understanding provided us with two different perspectives by which to explore meaning; trust and social capital. We have discussed how we approached re-designing *trust,* our second perspective explored how we might design the components of social capital.

Social capital - as discussed earlier - is the most powerful component of recovery capital, and most significantly for InHouse Records, it is the passport to social mobility, providing the *transition* from a ball of string network to a *bow tie* network and beyond.

Writing

Text: ALEKSANDAR VASILKOV

This is the third and final part of our conversation with professional stand-up comedian and voice-over artist Tom Ward. He delves deeply into the psychology of creative writing and gives some very valuable advice on starting out as a comedian, musician, or any other kind of performer.

INHOUSE: For people who are interested in getting into comedy after prison–what should they do to get into comedy on an amateur, maybe even semi-professional level? What are some sensible first steps?

TOM WARD: Angel Comedy is a very nice place to start. There is also a particularly supportive open mic in Stockwell. I recommend it because it's representative of the better end of the comedy experience at any level. It's called Comedy Virgins and it's at the Cavendish Arms in Stockwell. I went one week to watch, just to have a look, to see what it was like 'cause I was nervous about trying it. You take a friend and you have to stay all evening to support the other acts and so that everyone has an audience and the room is nice and full. It's a safe space. When you're new, you're going to be rubbish, probably. Some people are good straight away, which is actually horrible to see, as a comedian. You go, "Oh, you bastard! I was shit for ages!"

It's important to find somewhere where you feel safe to fail and to accept that failure.

Not being funny and maybe even offending people, will be part of your journey. You have to fuck up. And don't compare yourself to the legends, the greats, because they were going for 15-20 years before they became that well-known. Micky Flanagan wasn't famous for the first ten years, at least. And then that "Out Out" clip from Live at the Apollo made him a household name very quickly and he made 35 million in 2018. You've got to give yourself the time, you've got to allow yourself to be a beginner.

Give it a light touch. Go along, be rubbish for a few weeks, try out some stuff. If you feel like changing your sets, write a different set the following week. If you liked the set you were doing last week, have a look at it over the days after the gig. Always record it, so you can listen back. "What did they like? What did they not like?" And gradually, over time, you will find a way to learn. The audience teaches you what is working. They're always telling you information. Did they laugh? Did they stay quiet? Was it a good silence? Even if they weren't laughing, was that a good silence? Were they interested? Listen to the recording. If you got no laughs at all but you enjoyed it and you knew something felt good, come back the following week with what you've learned. Give yourself time. Start in a supportive environment. Don't go to some horrible Coliseum-style thing where the audience are told to heckle and you get booed off. It's not proper comedy. Start gently. Go to open mics where there's a supportive audience. There's a great quote from a book called The Artist's Way, and it says "Have the humility of the beginner". Accept that you're going to be rubbish. Make being rubbish part of the fun. "Oh, look how shit I am, this is fun"

If you admit that you're gonna be rubbish, then you're free. How can you possibly be the best? That takes years and years. If you enjoy it, go on a journey. Don't put pressure on yourself to be professional within three years. Ignore stories about people who did it very quickly. Concentrate on the people who took a long time. Make it fun, keep it fun, don't put pressure on it. It's a journey. If you've got a story you want to tell, then you want to tell it and that's it, there's no getting round it.

Rhythm

DUB

In the late 1960s Kingston-based music producers started issuing instrumental 'versions' on the B-side of reggae vocal releases. Pioneering sound engineers like Osbourne 'King Tubby' Ruddock and Lee 'Scratch' Perry began experimenting with these instrumental tracks with the use of studio effects such as echo, delay and reverb. Dub was a process of taking previously recorded material and modifying it, usually accentuating the rhythm section (drums and bass). The mixing desk became an instrument in itself and original recordings were reshaped into something new, usually with some or all of the vocals removed and a strong emphasis on the rhythm section. These 'dub' versions grew in popularity at the soundsystem dances and Deejays and selectors began requesting producers for more instrumental dubs, over which MCs could spit rhymes and deliver news.

This is such a crucial chapter in the history of popular and underground music, because it was these very innovations and the techniques introduced by Tubby and 'Scratch' Perry that sowed the seeds for 'remix' culture which is so prevalent today. Additionally, the notion of modifying previously recorded music to accentuate the drum and bass had never occurred before. Fans of Hip-Hop, House, Jungle, Drum and Bass, Grime, and any other bass heavy, lyrically-focused style of music here King Tubby and 'Scratch' Perry to thank.

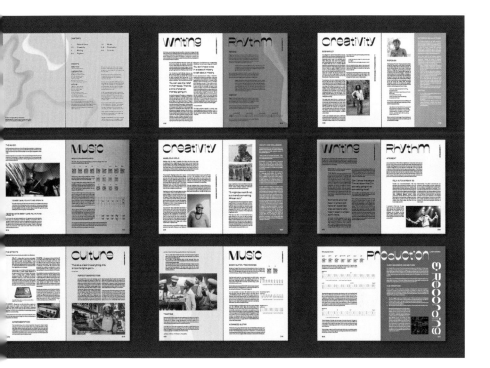

Magazine.

...eloped through our Social License, the multi-award winning, Aux Magazine, is a music ...culture journal designed exclusively for those in prison, by those in prison and ...ngside, those who have graduated from InHouse Records. Facilitated by the brilliant, ...e Holbrook, InHouse Managing Director and our incredible graphic designer, ...nah Lee.

...ugh meaningful collaboration and the antifragility of the Social License, we were able ...espond within three weeks of Covid-19 lockdown measures, in March 2020. For the rest ...20, Aux Magazine was the only full colour weekly content being delivered to over half ...e UK prisons at no cost to the prisons. We delivered over 70,000 copies to date and are ...producing the magazine for UK and USA prisons.

Re-designing social capital - Core Competencies

As part of the many conversations with stakeholders across the phenomena, I spent time speaking to a range of employers. I was particularly interested in the appetite of employers to hire people who possessed criminal records. Data from the Ministry of Justice shows that 27% of working-age adults have a criminal conviction. This increases to 33% when just looking at men[113]. However, a 2016 survey, commissioned by the Department of Work and Pensions, found that 50% of employers wouldn't consider employing someone with a criminal conviction.[114]

I spent time speaking to over fifty employers - all of whom had a track record of hiring people with criminal records. I was keen to understand what were the most important attributes they looked for in a prospective employee. I then spent time with a range of corporates - none of whom had a track record of hiring people with criminal records - and asked them the same question; what are the most important attributes they look for when selecting an employee?

Whilst there was some discrepancy between the two sets regarding the exact criteria - either qualifications or work experience, when it came to the interview phase both groups were in agreement. Beyond the initial criteria, employers want to know three things about the person they are hiring. Are they reliable? Are they willing to learn new skills? Will this person disrupt team harmony? In fact these three criteria could be viewed as fundamental core competencies: accountability, adaptability and communication.

Employers want to know if their potential employee can be depended upon, if they are willing to adapt and will they fit in? Of course, not every employer will approach hiring in this manner, but more employers are recognising that qualifications do not reveal the

[113] Ministry of Justice, Conviction Histories of Offenders, 2010 https://assets.publishing.service.gov.uk/media/5a7c98db40f0b65b3de09ea1/criminal-histories-bulletin.pdf

[114] https://www.refreshingacareer.com/list-of-companies-that-hire-ex-offenders-uk/#:~:text=According to data from the,t going unnoticed by businesses

mindset of the candidate. Qualifications do not reveal how a person behaves, communicates, learns and takes responsibility. A few employers told me they hired a candidate with less work experience and qualifications simply because they could see the candidate would fit in really well and appeared more reliable after a week's trial.

Recent research within His Majesty's Prison and Probation service recorded over 60% of men in prison, as having such severe communication difficulties, they are found in less than 10% of the general population.[115] However, in prison the men are expected to adhere to a range of nuanced communication requests from officers, prison staff and educators - the message is at risk of not being communicated at all.[116]

As a vehicle for designing meaning we began exploring these three competencies with a view to including them in our continuum.

Core Competency - Communication
"The single biggest problem in communication is the illusion that it has taken place.[117]" - George Bernard Shaw.

We all communicate, within the context of social capital however, communication is particularly concerned with our ability to present information to different audiences. The clarity to deliver a message, like a diplomat, and the active listening skills to discern if the message has been understood.

[115] Ella Gannon, Communication, Education and Speech Difficulties in the Criminal Justice System, 2020, Oxford Hub https://ohrh.law.ox.ac.uk/communication-education-and-speech-difficulties-in-the-criminal-justice-system/

[116] https://www.ncbi.nlm.nih.gov/pmc/articles/PMC10366709/ #:~:text=Communication Disorders1.-,Good communication is essential for resolving social conflicts, especially in,solving ability and increasing conflicts

[117] Irish Times, Conor Kenny, 9th November 2020

Factor of communication - Positive Verbal Communication
We established earlier the harshness of the language employed by our collaborators. For InHouse it became important to provide positive words framed in the learning tasks like how to become an artist or how to manage an artist. In both situations we explored scenarios of delivering difficult information clearly and compassionately. In practice this may look like the learner managing the studio diary. Managing the studio time slots at InHouse requires the learner to say no to people that have not booked a slot, providing the necessity for clear and kind communication.

With every task that needs to be completed (sometimes daily, always weekly) the learner needs to be able to convey if the task has been completed, and if not, why not. The importance isn't placed on task completion, but on communication. The clearer and more honest the communication, the more growth in dialogic speech. Essentially communication became a feature of everyone's work regardless of the actual task.

Danish footballing legend Michael Laudrup - considered to be one of the games greatest players - was reflecting on Johan Cruyff's strengths as a manager - Laudrup shared Cruyff's ability to deliver complex themes with utter simplicity. Positive verbal communication explores the ability to refine our words and communicate simply what complex thoughts we may be feeling. Communicating effectively using intonation, pitch, tone and cadence.

Whilst exploring our cohort at InHouse Records it became apparent that verbal communication was rarely positive. Through the art of songwriting and communicating about the aspiration of music, we were able to stretch conversation to new areas, foreign places, where we explored complexity, feelings and thoughts, as we sought to communicate those feelings in song. Speaking about those feelings was not possible before, but speaking about them as part of songwriting somehow made it possible. Finally by inviting people from the music industry to attend workshops, the learners would observe how a label manager would communicate and begin to adopt similar approaches. Validation through modelling professional behaviour.

Factor of communication - Positive Non-Verbal Communication
Often our body language can reveal more about how we are feeling
than our words can. Have you ever asked someone how they are
feeling and not been satisfied with their answer? You know that they
are not 'fine', and actually they are quite upset about something but
they are just not saying it. Non-verbal communication can sometimes
reveal everything.

We communicate through posture, facial expressions, and hand
gestures. Our ability to understand and interpret other people's body
language can help identify unspoken issues or feelings. Without a
clear understanding of non-verbal communication, we might be saying
one thing and demonstrating something altogether different.
Communication through positive body language represents a critical
part of combining meaning into speaking, maintaining eye contact and
holding attention.

For InHouse Records, inviting professionals from the music industry
to attend showcases in prison allowed us to practice and develop our
non-verbal and verbal communication. Performing on stage presented
the opportunity to improve posture, moving to an open and relaxed
stance and away from a disinterested slouching positions. Incidentally,
inviting friends and family to showcases in prison resulted in a
phenomena that had been missing in most of the interactions thus far -
genuine joy. The men would smile when their families would visit for a
concert - and smiling, we learnt, was a natural enhancer of non-verbal
communication. We would sometimes exaggerate our awareness of
body language by asking the artists to perform their songs without
lyrics. Essentially the artists would act out the track without using
words. We would then ask the rest of the cohort to guess what the
track was about. Communication when made clear through positive
verbal communication and positive non-verbal communication can
reinforce the meaning of a message.

Factor of communication - Positive Written Communication

For many in prison, writing is a significant barrier and in the interests of establishing a safe and enabling environment, we never pressure the men to write things down. When I first began visiting prisons in the UK, spending time with the men, I made a conscious decision not to write anything down, as I was mindful of not creating any barriers. The person with pen and paper carefully taking notes may not only be assuming power or judgement which is bad enough anyway, but it does not help build trust - in fact it raises suspicion.

The process of using a mental note book severely tested my abilities to recall small and large details on a daily basis. However I perfected a way of remembering at least ten key elements and twenty sub-elements every day. It is incredible how much the mind can store - I was always profoundly moved and inspired by the incredible story of Michel Thomas[118], the famed linguist, and decorated war veteran, whom, during World War II, whilst being held in a prisoner of war camp, was able to keep a *mental* day diary. Thomas' day diary contained details such as the weather, notable conversations he had with different prisoners and anything he may have eaten. What made the diary remarkable was his ability to recall the detail of every single day of his incarceration.

Over the course of the following months, I was able to store numerous meetings and multiple conversations all in my mind. After almost a year of going in and out of prison - and culminating with the full launch of InHouse Records - I asked the men their permission to bring in a notebook that would help me write down ideas for their songs and support them on their individual journeys.

Not only did they all agree to me bringing in a note book, but they asked if they could have notebooks too - together we collaborated to design InHouse Records notebooks and printed over 1,000 copies within the first few years.

---

[118] Christopher Robbins, The Test of Courage - a biography of Michel Thomas, 2000, Arrow

Writing used to be something that had connotations with school and failure, suddenly it had become cool - associated with a record label and expression.

Factor of communication - Positive Visual Communication
Rituals rely on some form of icon or visual representation, therefore promoting visual literacy is an imperative facet of communication. For many in prison, visual communication provides the easiest vehicle to making a connection, and the role of design in this instance was to ensure we were creating the conditions for visual communication to carry positive meaning, and perhaps re-establish meaning. Visuals can aid the understanding of a message, often messages where meaning cannot be made possible by words alone. The use of imagery can additionally help bridge the gap between the messages meaning and the words, especially when the audience may come with diverse needs and from differing backgrounds.

Visual communication can feel safest for those who struggle to read and write, and for many of the men, visual communication would enable quicker decision making. Songs could be drawn with icons or images, instead of words - this allows the artist to use the images as rubber scaffolding to support the structure of the song without feeling the restriction of concrete words. In practice, this could look like simple stick drawings that represented a powerful narrative.

Similar to Kanji - which are Chinese origin characters that have been adapted to the Japanese language - the men would create characters that possessed the scope for the artist to interpret the imagery how they saw fit, depending on their mood on any given day. Positive visual communication is not just a stepping stone to a wider more nuanced communication, but an essential enrichment of our language. Hope has its own set of semiotics, as do endings, transitions and beginnings.

Above. From left Jim Chancellor, Judah Ar[...] Neil Sartorio and Nic[...] DeLeon. Without thes[...] professional and compassionate collab[...] there would be no InH[...] Records - alliances ac[...] space, time and cultur[...]

Left. Neil Sartorio an[...] Lance Harris - the [...] terquarista of the just[...] system, at an InHous[...] Records showcase in [...] 2019.

bove. Re-designing meaning through
pressions of creativity - InHouse
ssion in HMP.

ight. InHouse Records graduate - in
nversation with Jamie Franklin
ad of Artist Relations at Roland UK.

Core Competency - Accountability

"It's not only what we do, but what we do not, that makes us accountable[119]" - Molière

Accountability is a behaviour that was deeply inherent in the role of the Medieval Guild craftsman. When we are able to value our work we become answerable to ourselves before we become answerable to anyone else. When we are able to value what we do, the role of a manager can change from the caricature of an oppressive boss, to one of a positive professional coach.

Being answerable and responsible for our outcomes, regardless of success or failure is to own the actions that determine our life. For the early collaborators of InHouse Records and for all future learners, the word accountability often triggered negative feelings. The deep set relationship with accountability is often similar to the overbearing manager, where accountability has been distorted and viewed as a close relative of punishment.

By re-designing trust and seeking to provide rich meaning into harsh words, accountability could be viewed as something altogether different, not as punishment, but actually a sanctuary. An internal place where we are able to be true to ourselves - doing what we say and enjoying the peace that brings.

Factor of accountability - Craftsmanship

Developing a sense of pride in all we do is perhaps a difficult concept to embrace if doing things well was never modelled throughout our childhood. I certainly did not have any of my primary relationships modelled well, in fact, they were modelled in rather damaging ways, so much so, that taking care to build a relationship with kindness, care and love were attributes I had to learn much later in life.

Usually, growing up in particularly challenging circumstances can make an individual feel they are on the outside of society. I know I certainly felt like a second class citizen growing up, these feelings can

---

[119] Moière, Tartuffe, 1981, Prentice Hall UK

make a person feel *less than* other people. It took me a long time to realise that living on the fringes of society is never *less than* but actually *more than*. Having to navigate a personal journey whilst being on the edges of society requires more skill, resilience, determination and creativity.

At InHouse by giving space for the learners to reflect, we are in effect making each story a valuable item, like a gem stone that needs to be handled carefully. Choices need to be made regarding how to treat the development of a song. This process instills care and when we care about what we make, we are able to make things well.

In this sense, the collaborators at InHouse Records concern themselves with taking pride in the music they are creating, being open to improve not just each song they are working on, but improving their knowledge of the process - always demonstrating a considerable deployment of time and effort towards their projects. Craft is a flexible approach to adopt as it can be applied to all things once the approach is made familiar. Through developing the craft of songwriting for example, the craft of becoming a better parent, partner or friend can be visualised more easily.

Factor of accountability - Time
Being accountable for what we make, (craftsmanship) can be a starting point as we explore a journey towards responsibility. Being responsible for time has been potentially the hardest factor of accountability to foster within our conversations. In the early days of InHouse Records, a few of the collaborators would always arrive late, even though everyone was coming from the same wings of the prison.

Many of the collaborators likened timekeeping to feelings of being judged or having a penny pinching boss. We were able to ensure that our sessions included guest speakers from the industry, and song clinics with established artists, or even family shows. The more engaging we made the sessions the more the learners were keen to arrive on time in case they missed out on anything.

After operating for a few months almost all of our learners were arriving as soon as they were possibly allowed. We would have one to one artist development sessions for which they themselves would organise with InHouse staff. Indeed the studio time, the time given to actually record the songs that have been refined and developed with an engineer, would be managed by the learners themselves. In effect this is an example of *blocking their own scene*, as learners would create schedules that the rest of the cohort would engage with; managers booking studio time for their artists, for example. We worked hard to create a space where time was valued, a space where we operated in both Chronos and Kairos - the hours and minutes and the depth of relationship, in time and outside of time.

Factor of accountability - Professionalism
Accountability with regards to what we make, (craftsmanship) and time, combine to support the elements of professional behaviour.

Within the music industry professionalism focuses on accumulating the gathered learning of verbal and non verbal communication, craftsmanship and time management, all applied towards specific scenarios like composing an email, attending an interview or calling a meeting for example. Ultimately ensuring that clear and professional articulation takes place throughout.

The value of professionalism is highlighted even more so when it can be de-coupled from having to constantly feel enthused. Some of the learners would rely on the *buzz* of the creative process to talk about their work, which was absolutely fine when the process was yielding lots of songs, however when they were less productive it became much harder to generate a *buzz* and thus talking became tough.

Through exploring a professional behaviour towards music, the learners were able to talk about their music even when they were not feeling productive. Not being reliant on a *buzz* of productivity, enabled clarity of articulation. A factor of being able to communicate professionally was the articulation of the creative process. In doing so, the *buzz* was seen as a by-product of the process, not integral.

Core Competency - Adaptability
"Those who cannot change their minds cannot change anything [120]" -
George Bernard Shaw.

Adaptability is not just the ability to deal with change, but the art of learning, and paying particular attention to understanding how we learn.

For many of the participants at InHouse Records, learning to learn can be a liberating process. However the designer must also be open to challenge their own ideals of what knowledge is. As we explored earlier, whilst discussing *respect*, we need to find alternative ways of acknowledging achievement - being open to different forms of knowledge. Perhaps now more than ever having the room to accept different forms of knowledge should be welcomed. Is a person less knowledgable because they cannot read or write, yet they may have amassed unique life knowledge from living through super challenging circumstances. The designer must be adept at identifying new ways of learning that can enrich a diverse understanding of knowledge, especially embodied knowledge that remains firmly outside the purview of AI algorithms. What we know but cannot easily articulate - semi-solid in state - may be more important to our society that even before.

Change in general however should be carefully nurtured and thus, adaptability requires a safe and enabling arena to be explored. Adaptability will always be driven by curiosity and therefore, the designer should be mindful of the power that aspirations possess in the transitional collaboration of any initiative. We are going to learn that which we want to learn, thus, learning requires appetite that begets aspiration. How we deal with change in life, is an immense part of coping positively.

---

[120] George Bernard Shaw, Everybody's Political What's What, 1944, Constable

Factor of adaptability - Resourcefulness

If we are to encourage and identify new forms of intelligence and celebrate embodied learning, we must be open to designing the spaces that clearly visualise new phenomena. We must see opportunity where others do not.

When we started InHouse Records our attitude to make the label work with limited resources was not just an exercise in positivity, but a realisation that we did not have the time to wait six months for security to clear all the equipment needed - we are in a race to outpace the clock speed of the phenomena, because in this instance speed is justice. Modelling that behaviour from the beginning resulted in the men being able to make do with whatever tools and equipment we had at hand. Subsequently the learners become less reliant on tools and used resourcefulness to achieve their outcomes.

Factor of adaptability - Resistance

As mentioned earlier, curiosity is a factor in a learning journey. However we must work together to build resistance if sustained engagement of the learning journey is to be realised.

Learning thrives when there is a degree of resistance, this is most obviously personified in the gaming culture. What good would a game be if it could be mastered in one sitting? The point of gaming is to grow an adaptive mindset, learning from previous attempts that didn't work in order to improve and progress through new levels. Resistance, when nurtured positively can promote a growth mindset.

Has the skill of designing resistance become a forgotten art? I have observed many designers who are so concerned with seamless simplicity that their user does not have the opportunity to wrestle, challenge, or be curious enough to progress. I was visiting a friend in London recently and we had agreed to meet in a cafe. About twenty minutes before arriving, the battery on my phone died. After a few moments I began to experience and feel sensations that were almost foreign to me, although not quite - I realised that I had forgotten what it's like to be lost. We don't get lost anymore. I certainly recall a time in my youth when all I needed was an A-Z of London (map) and friendly banter to drive across London visiting friends. The feeling of being lost, heightens all the other senses. Lost in London, immediately my brain was learning street names, taking in the colours of shops fronts, acknowledging the flow of traffic - I was making myself familiar with the landscape. In order to make anything, we need to make sense - I arrived at the cafe, early and with the journey knowledge etched in my mind. Sometimes I now find myself exiting a London Underground station and choosing to ignore the map on my phone as I allow myself to be lost, so that I can find myself once more.

At InHouse Records, the arena of music provides natural resistance - everyone's second song will be better than their first and by their fifth or sixth song, they can all tell the difference of what *better* sounds like. For the musician, resistance comes in the form of being able to maintain a beat on the drums, or play a variety of chords on guitar, or move from one chord to another quickly enough to maintain the tempo of the song. The designer must ensure that resistance is always considered when exploring engagement, as the personal achievement through resistance begets confidence and increases appetite for further adaptability.

Ultimately the more resistance, natural or self imposed like turning my phone off, will develop the appetite for life long learning.

Factor of adaptability - Application
Learning that remains theoretical is vulnerable to being forgotten. The application of learning therefore becomes the crucible by which we are able to make sense of what we have learnt. Sometimes we make things in order to figure out what we learnt. This is prevalent when we are creating something from our embodied knowledge, sometimes what we know is so deeply placed inside of us that our best articulation might be to make something. Application in this sense becomes a crucial exercise in manifesting what we know - yet cannot articulate.

Application however, can also be a way of embedding what we know through making something, we apply knowledge to an artefact. The theory of a particular dish only becomes truly known when we actually prepare the meal, and only then does it fully become applied knowledge - and what we know, we can never forget.

The designer must understand where best to sequence the application of knowledge. At inHouse Records staff model this behaviour towards the learners, in fact all the competencies discussed are part of a modelled behaviour for all our staff. For the designer however, it is of huge importance to model the behaviour that has been curated, which brings us back to the very first movement. The socially driven designer, in pursuing an interior journey of personal change, can be best equipped for the exterior journey of societal impact.

Meaning and Measuring
We began this section by seeking to establish a way by which the designer can re-introduce meaning to language that has become harsh from the challenging conditions that fostered it. We have discussed the dimensions of trust and explored how we might re-design respect in order to achieve greater equity and therefore, greater meaning. We also explored the intricate formats of communication, accountability and adaptability - the trinity of core competencies. We discovered that a fresh approach to accessing the competencies was essential because in its raw format each one has the potential to trigger negative consequences - leading to past trauma. The designer, therefore, must explore the endings of these relationships thoroughly before designing better transitions and beginnings. To that end, we have established fresh approaches to communication, accountability and adaptability. We discovered a symbiotic relationship between the core competencies; whereby adaptability fuels accountability and simultaneously enhances communication. The development of core competencies makes it easier for someone to articulate their accountability and therefore taking responsibility of their own life. As a result learning becomes more straightforward as the individual can communicate with clarity and appetite, what they know and that which they do not.

An unexpected phenomena that took place across all the components of the core competencies is that learners developed a *group* accountability. The more an individual took responsibility for their own actions, the more they become aware of others and in doing so, were moving towards active citizenship. In some cases, depending on the individual, this could grow into positive leadership skills.

Our primary challenge was to define meaning through words, whereby the world to which a man belongs to, can become the world which belongs to man. However our secondary challenge was to define value through impact, whereby the landscape of businesses is less about selling to people and more about serving people. It's important to underline that changing the face of business was not the primary remit of my practice, indeed InHouse Records was born from a Social License, a conversation.

We cannot do anything without affecting everything else and the designer must be aware of the fresh cadence a new conversation across space, time and culture may have. Of course InHouse Records has to provide measurable outcomes, but we have ensured these outcomes are focused on the competencies. Our competency matrix that measures growth in communication, accountability and adaptability is used by many other organisations by which to capture the development of social capital.

InHouse Records would not have been possible without the creation of a Social License - a collaborative entity that can host conversations of change across time. However InHouse Records isn't the Social License it is merely an artefact of the Social License.

The by-product of the Social Licence in prison is InHouse Records, Aux Magazine and Lucky13's. I have mentioned Aux Magazine earlier however Lucky13's is a truly brilliant resource that like InHouse and Aux could not have been created without the Social License.

RHYME

Improve your lyrics

HALF RHYMES

EMINEM – THE WAY I AM

"And since birth I've been cursed with this curse to just curse/and just blurt this berserk and bizarre shit that works"

These are half rhymes – they're not exact but they're a great tool for giving you more options for words. Half rhymes with Cursed worse, shirts, hurts, blurts, works, Turks, converts, births, asserts, clerks, skirts, deserts, alerts, jerks, quirks, inverts, diverts.

Find words that fit the feeling behind your lyrics.

CONTINUUM   *Issue One*

LUCKY 13

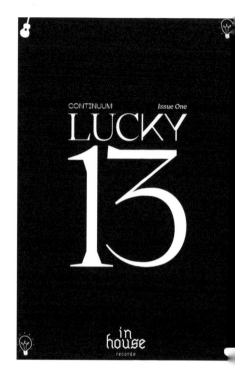

in house
records

LYRIC

Word flow for your bars

LYRICAL TOOLBOX

SYSTEM

Similar words to system are; Arrangement, entity, fixed-order, ideology, machine, philosophy, regularity, rule, scheme, structure, status quo, totality, method, procedure, approach, plan, framework, pattern, modus operandi.

Opposite words to system are; cog, part, fraction, disorder, chaos, confusion, mess, violence, disarrangement, disarray, mayhem, jumble, bedlam, dismay, disruption, disorientation

Using different words, help your bars sound different. Explore different ways to say what you want to say?

RHY — THM

Learn rhythm. Tap rhythms. Use Rhythms in your writing, in your flow in your music. Just like the unit to measure money in the UK is Sterling, with the smallest unit being a penny. So Poetry has it's own way of measuring rithm. The unit is called "feet" and the first "feet" or unit we are exploring is called an iamb like the penny, it's a very small unit.

iamb = unstressed / stressed

Imagine a word like enjoy. You don't stress the first part En, but the second part is where you put the emphasis or stress JOY.

Other exmaples of "iamb":

en-JOY, be-LONG, de-GREE, re-PEAT, e-VOLVE, ex-CITE, in-TENSE.

The rhythm of these words goes

buh-BUH

Try to use these words to come up with a phrase, where the rhythm repeats for effect.

Example: be-LONG, be STRONG, we MOVE, in SONG, and WHO, is ON, the TUNE, we RUN

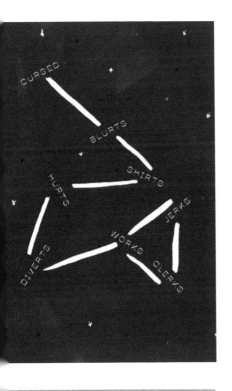

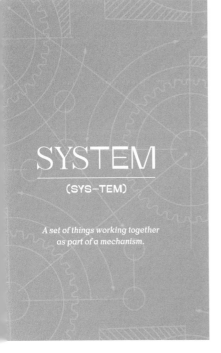

SYSTEM

(SYS–TEM)

*A set of things working together
as part of a mechanism.*

Lucky13's.

*An artefact developed through the same
Social License that birthed InHouse
Records. A weekly deck of cards
designed to replace distance learning.
Formed and informed by a Neurodiverse
community. Learners are able to build
their own curriculum on a weekly basis,
working towards an accredited
qualification. Cards feature a word side
and an image side - intentionally moving
away from exercise books towards
meaningful communication.*

*Designed by the amazing Sarah Nolloth
and the incredible Ollie Mac.*

Society driven design creates an inseparability across all the stakeholders. The audience ca
identify between InHouse Records graduates, staff or volunteers. There is a natural inextri
link when genuine collaboration occurs. Since 2018 InHouse graduates have organised ove
live music events, including performances at Brighton Festival and twice at Latitude festiva
Our indivisible connection has been a constant theme of all our performances.

in house RECORDS

PRESENTS

A seated night of live performance for your entertainment, giving you the realest expression through music and spoken word.

3 FLIPZ, BABYJAI, KANDI GOLD, CAROLINE, CHERRALYN, C.ROOTS, LEONSIDE, MALIKAI GRAY, MS RANYE, NURSE, PARIS LOVECHILD, HOSTED BY SMITTY

8-10PM · FREE ENTRY 7TH APRIL 2022 BRIXTON STUDIOS SW9 8LB

POETIC JUSTICE

LATITUDE

nhouse Records

Lucky13's is a new way of delivering distance learning, especially to those who find themselves on a neurodiverse spectrum in prison. Lucky13's provides recognised accredited qualifications through a weekly set of non-linear distance learning cards. A curriculum that can be completely designed by the prisoner, through choice architecture. Lucky13's has been formed and informed by neurodiverse collaborators across the prison system, innovating education through the use of colour, a reduced word count and print safe fonts.

The Social License should not be seen as a way of legitimising existing businesses as was the case in the early twentieth century - applying it as a bolt on. The modern Social License should be seen as a legitimate vehicle that can birth socially impactful business and charitable ventures. Re-ordering how we create the right to operate before, and not after we have established a profit making business. InHouse Records embeds the skills to design better conversations, providing all with a freedom to travel, and the confidence to deploy newly acquired skills across different networks - demonstrated through a re-offending rate of less than 1%.[121]

InHouse Records successfully champions the space, through meaningful conversations to travel from a ball of string network to *bow tie* and *daisy* networks, through a re-designing of respect, communication, accountability and adaptability in order to build trust.

InHouse Records has grown from a record label to become a label for change, increasing from one prison in the UK, to multiple in the UK and USA. InHouse Records extends its remit, continuing to work outside of prison where perhaps our graduates need the most support, re-connecting with a cold society through positive relationships. Our team of staff, graduates and volunteers organise gigs, showcases and festival appearances where everyone performs. For many attending the showcases outside of prison, it is difficult to tell which of the performers on stage are InHouse Records graduates and which are volunteers who have never actually been to prison - indeed this is an

---

[121] InHouse Records NESTA Reporting -Graduate Engagement Post Release 2023
https://www.inhouserecords.org/about

important design feature - because quite frankly, it doesn't matter if you can't tell who's who. What unites us is our desire to want to see better ways of being human, that seems more important than conforming to *an us and them* narrative. These dualistic ways of thinking can bring division, even whilst in the process of trying to do something positive. Our showcases are intentionally ambiguous, just like our subjunctive conversations, they should remain open, inclusive and focus on our humanity not any social ordering of our divisions - designing conversations across space, time and culture.

...use has grown from
...aborative
...rsation to a record
...and from a record
...o a label for
...e. Together we
...e-defined respect,
...fied meaning and
...ust.

...: James Walker

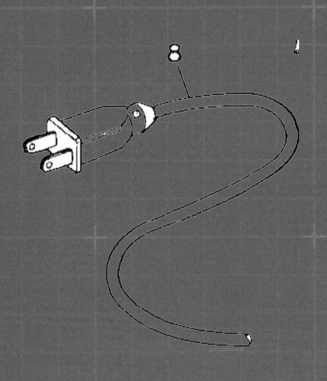

Transitioning

Everything is in flux.
Building a practice that can transition always made sense to me.

Socially driven design is a transitional practice - a journey interrupted
by the whispers of new beginnings and the grief of respectful endings.

The Social License is an iterative dialogue - a conversation across
space time and culture, about creating the environment for change.

Everything discussed in this book has either been about the
transitional practice or the iterative conversation.
Socially driven design or the Social License.

Designer

If the designer cannot understand themselves, then meaningful
collaboration with others becomes impossible. The designer must
embark on an interior journey, familiarising themselves with who they
are and who they wish to become. Discovering chambers within the
heart where values can be carved and lakes of understanding that
ripple across comprehension.

Design is neither truthful nor deceptive - the socially driven designer
has a civic responsibility to define design and establish a relationship
with it that can form and inform their transitional practice.
Transitional, because everything is in flux, and the designer always
finds themselves trailing the clock speed of the phenomena.
The most precious gift we have is time. The designer who seeks to
contribute to the world, must sacrifice theirs - the Chronos hours
needed to build the Kairos relationships.

For all to be able to contribute to society driven design, the designer
must be able to reach all in conversation. Becoming accustom to the
poet, the diplomat, the surveyor and the architect - all the diverse roles
within the Cruyff inspired total *design* playing field. By reaching all in

conversation, the designer can free the maker in us all - as all can participate in a conversation across space, time and culture. The transitional practice of the society driven designer is formed by values, understanding and methods. Values and understanding yield conversational literacy. The interior journey provides external fluency as the designer becomes proficient in the craft of value exchanges, rituals and dialogic speech. Indeed both the interior and exterior journey equip the designer to master the language of loss and endings.

The society driven designer must make the familiar unfamiliar, by strengthening Plath's beating slack drum that has lost meaning, and awaken our senses by a fresh language that appears strange and wonderful. Re-ordering that which we know to prevent half hearted experiences.

Conversation
Modern work no longer possesses the social architecture to host meaningful long term collaboration. We require a legitimatised space to anchor conversations of change across space, time and culture. The Social License is a proactive vehicle for change and a catalyst to defining meaning and breaking division.

Conversations with License holders creates an inseparability across all the stakeholders, as we move away from dualistic thinking. At our gigs performed by InHouse Records outside of prison, the audience members cannot identify between our graduates from prison and our staff or volunteers. There is a natural inseparability when genuine collaboration occurs over time. In the same way Manet created an inseparable quality between his art and the audience, so too must the socially driven designer.

Society driven design requires us to see more than just the person standing before us, but the harsh experiences that live behind them, the profoundly painful experiences that live further back still, and the brutal language that perpetually surrounds them.

Meaningful collaboration requires us to see behind the person standing in front of us. Behind the person with a knife stands the person who sold them a knife, and the employer who didn't give them that much needed first job, and the cabinet minister who decided that their school was in a postcode that didn't warrant additional funding, and the owner who closed down the manufacturing factory where they may have worked, and the government that decided to cut benefits[122]. All these people stand behind the person before us.

The designer must be able to look back far enough in order to see themselves - our interdependence and our accountability - for many this is why they have become socially driven designers.

The designer must apply the same vision to systems, choosing to see behind the system of systems in order to understand the whole and not merely the part that everyone knows. My friend Thomas Horton at the Ministry of Justice was able to launch the brilliant Grand Avenues initiative that features place based probation. The groundbreaking work was made possible because of Thomas' complete understanding of the process. The designer who operates outside of a Social License will rarely be afforded the time to understand the whole system and more than likely be shown a process that takes place regularly across an institution. Typical is not all. Typical may not even be half. Typical is often the process that's used the most - the process used so often it has its own template. Collaboration across space, time and culture, permits the designer to see beyond the templates and typical processes. The Social License can breathe fresh air into tired systems and in doing so launch initiatives of imagination and change.

The Social License
For the last twenty years I have been hosting conversations across two Social Licenses. Conversations that are not tethered to a project but conversations that have birthed many initiatives. The Social License is an iterative conversation that operates at the speed of a transitional practice. I imagine these conversations to reveal glimpses of Medieval

---

[122] https://www.dannydorling.org/?page_id=1047

Guilds as they gift the space for community 'genius', collaboration and hope, the real kind of hope - the kind that provides a liberation of creativity in confinement.

Society driven design brings all the components for a collaborative conversation together like an exploded drawing.

The Social License is an emergent process, and as such I have been keen to resist a didactic approach to formalising its use. I have spent more time sharing the values and methods that help shape our understanding of the process, than actually specify how one should or should not use it. I hope you can see the difference and embrace the License in the spirit it has been shared. The design space has been heavily serviced with a high a degree of functionality that perhaps creates an unhealthy dependency on tools. Do you really want a Social License toolkit? I am sure you can exercise the agency and choice to establish your own License.

My hope is that you will establish a Social License across areas of society that mean something to you. Create a Social License with your colleagues, choose a phenomena to explore and begin! Conversations will naturally reveal collaborators and some may become License holders. The approach to License holders has been adaptive. A few License holders chose to become collaborators to launch InHouse Records. What's the difference you may ask? Collaborators for InHouse, are interested in developing InHouse and only InHouse. License holders are enjoying the conversations too much and we continue meeting regularly to explore differing areas. The conversations, as I have mentioned earlier in the book, are ambiguous and vague, but never meaningless. In my experience the conversation topic is rarely chosen formally but more or less emerges from the moment we greet each other.

The License can also provide you with a legitimacy that running a few co-creation workshops doesn't quite give you. In addition when looking to launch an initiative, informing an organisation that you have an active Social License offers far more validation. The Social License always provides individual value. The skills developed in the art of conversations become the portable understanding that can be applied in network growth, social mobility and agency - the resources for personal development. You may choose to document your License in some kind of written format. I never have. However, explore what serves your License holders best.

If you do choose to move forward with your License, (and I really hope you do), what is most important is that you are actually doing something of value, which is no small thing in today's climate. I think we all find it hard to be acknowledged or affirmed for exploring design in challenging circumstances, simply because design does not naturally live in these space and thus we may be prone to feeling isolated. Do not worry. We are never alone. We are part of nature, we are part of our neighbourhoods and we are a member of society.

Socially driven design requires less of our minds and more of our hearts. When we give ourselves over to doing what we are passionate about, we will find ourselves journeying with our own tribe. People who we can trust, who can be like mirrors to us and we to them, reflecting honesty and truth.

Aristotle[123] believed that moral excellence comes about as a result of habit. We become 'just' by doing 'just acts', temperate by doing temperate acts, brave by doing brave acts. The process of doing something, and doing it frequently, develops our ability to improve, to do it better, to do it well.

Whatever barriers you believe are preventing you from starting a Social License, according to Aristotle can be bridged by simply starting a Social License. We all have a practice; we all have values, skills and understanding, that can further articulate our practice and in doing so we become naturally fluent in the language of endings, transitions and beginnings.

---

[123] Aristotle, Greek Library, Loeb Classical Library - Original 400-300BC, Ethics

InHouse Records showcase in HMP 2018

InHouse Records

At InHouse Records we were able to see prisoners and prison staff collaborate in profound ways. We learnt that an enemy is only someone who is not yet understood. Factors of diminished time, lack of respect, old organisational structures and lost meaning in conversations prevented the development of the collaborative process.

We shaped an environment where the prisoner can be seen as a person; the criminal archetype can become a creative architect of their own life. Meaning restored through words that can inspire transition from archetype to architect.

All things end, but the ending of something isn't always the ending of everything. One of the first people I ever met in prison was called S, who turned out to be a founding collaborator of InHouse Records. Early on in the process, I asked S what he wanted to achieve through InHouse, he said "to make something that can live outside these walls."

The first song that was ever written at InHouse Records was written by S and was titled *These Walls*[124].

What do they see beside my flaws?
How can I prove, I ain't the same guy I was,
And show, that there's a life behind these doors,
Could I ever live outside these walls?

But don't give up on me yet please
In case I don't make it,
Tell my people don't forget me
Tell my brothers don't turn out to be a next 'me'
Tell my mum I got her, coz she's the only one that gets me.

Lyrics S - Copyright InHouse Records 2017.

---

[124] Lyrics - SP, These Walls, 2017 InHouse Records

Total Design

We all live in a world of taxes and injustice, a world that can be harsh, and sometimes cold. We all live in a world where poverty exists and loved ones pass away. We all live in a world where cars breakdown and systems crash. We all live in a world with people, some get married, some get divorced.

At the same time we all have a world that lives in us.
The world that lives in us keeps the memories of loved ones alive forever. The world that lives in us houses our dreams, imagination and fears. In the world that lives in me, I always score the winner in the Cup Final. In the world that lives in me, my children are with me wherever I go.

We all live in the world.
We all have a world that lives in us.

We can make sense of the world that lives in us by speaking into the world we live in. Before we design anything, we are designing conversations - ones that communicate between the world we live in and the world that lives in us.

The world we live in is the everyday.
The world that lives in us, is sacred.

We are designing conversations across the everyday and scared.
From holy wine to tap water, with communion and community.

Design is spiritual and material.

A conversation, across space, time and culture, between the world we live in and the world that lives in us.

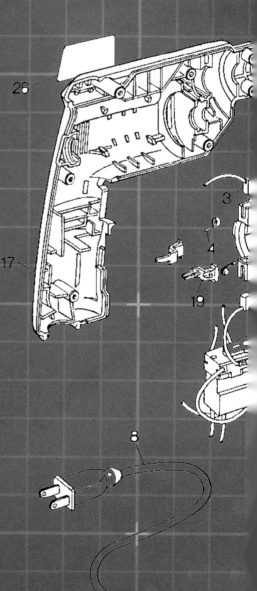

Society Driven Design brings all the components for collaborative conversation together, like the truth of an exploded drawing.

Everything falls into place. Collaborations that will continue far beyond the projects that we will make together - revealing the art of the Social License.

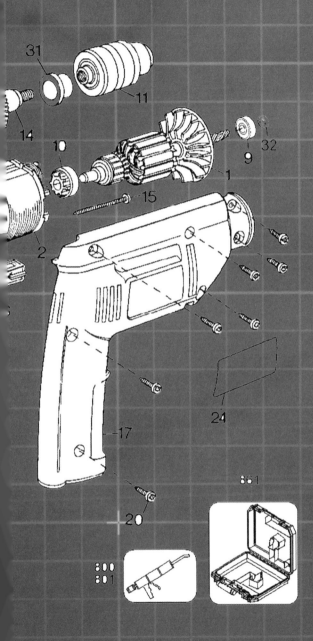

31

11

14

32

10

1

2

15

17

24

20

861

800
801

Respect
I salute every single one of you who aspires to make change in this world, every designer, entrepreneur and change-maker who is willing to sacrifice their time - you are brilliant!

For those who are going to start a Social License in whatever phenomena - I am thrilled! Much respect to you and wishing you all the success in hosting beautiful conversations across space, time and culture.

The Social License is not mine to give away, it has always been yours. My gift has been sharing it with you.

Please do let me know what you make together.

Every blessing,

J.

the reflection at folies-bergère

what happens if i cannot recognise?
i stare and discern
but don't see
the reflection at folies-bergère
a mirror looks back on me

bleary slits split in two
suffocating and encircled
i swim beneath graves
to get to you

patterns snap
we exhale relief in
gaps,

but,

oh,
our unburnt ashes
ablaze and tangled in two

our idyllic blasphemy
echos of reality
with myriad crimes
and whispers of our identity

what happens when i recognise?
the moment i see
i stare into a mirror
and it shows me

my reflection at folies-bergère

Tallulah Mae Armani